$even $ecrets of the Millionaires

Stuart Goldsmith

Copyright © Stuart Goldsmith 2001

First published in the United Kingdom by:
Medina Ltd, 230 Peppard Road, Emmer Green,
Reading, Berkshire, UK, RG4 8UA

First Published June 2001

Kindle Edition
Published by NS WebMarketing June 2011

All rights reserved. No reproduction, copy or transmission of this publication may be made without written permission. No paragraph of this publication may be reproduced, copied or transmitted without written permission, or in accordance with the Copyright Act 1956 (amended).

This book is sold for entertainment purposes only, and the author, publishers or distributors are not responsible for any actions taken as a result of reading this book.

Acknowledgements

The source material for the philosophic discussions in this book originated in Ayn Rand's philosophy 'Objectivism.'

Grateful thanks to Barbara Sher for providing the inspiration for chapter three.

Contents

Do You Sincerely Want to be Rich   1

Belief in Your Right to Retain Wealth   15

It All Starts With a Dream   38

You Must Have a Plan   57

You Need Discipline   69

You Must be Prepared to Pay the Price   81

You Must Take Firm, Decisive Action   93

You Must Know When to Stop   112

The Secret of Happiness   126

Chapter One
Do You Sincerely Want to be Rich?

By 'rich' I mean in excess of ten million pounds.

These days you are not rich if you have one million. Although not pocket-change, a million in the bank would merely allow you to live in moderate comfort for the rest of your days. You would have to be careful with money. You could not be extravagant. One million in disposable capital would give you around £50,000 a year in salary after tax, which is a lot less than a good company director gets. If you took this salary, the million would slowly be eaten away by inflation until it was worth just £350,000 (today's buying power) in about fifteen years. Hardly a king's ransom, I think you'll agree.

One million pounds buys you a decent house in the South of England, that's all. After you've bought the house, all the money has gone and there would not be a penny left to furnish it, pay the bills or for living expenses. No, the days are long gone when becoming a millionaire was a crazy dream. Being a millionaire is not what it used to be. A millionaire in 1900 would have the equivalent of one hundred million pounds in today's money!

Ten million though....ah, now we're talking sensible money. Ten million today is worth the same as one million used to be worth in the 1950's. A millionaire really *was* someone before 1950.

With ten million in the bank you can spend about £250,000 a year (£20,000 a month) and still have modest growth on your capital, but you would be in the bottom echelons of the wealthy, knocking for admittance to the fringes of their outer circle. Interestingly, if your ten million was ever reduced to one million, you would be described as 'flat broke' by your new circle of friends. People would talk about you in hushed and sympathetic voices. They would turn away and cough politely as you walked into a room. This would not be snobbery; just embarrassment and pity for one reduced to such poverty.

"He's down to his last million! Oh the poor, *poor* dear boy!"

The point here is perspective.

When you've had ten or a hundred million, this level of wealth seems normal for you. To be down to your last million really is flat broke - an horrific state to be in.

In contrast, when you have an overdraft and exist on a pittance, then a paltry £10,000 feels like a staggeringly large pile of cash - a gleaming mountain of gold. And a million? Well, this seems unimaginable; a sum of money which simply cannot be held in the mind, it is so vast.

It is this sense of perspective which aids the rich person and hampers the poor. If you have made a few million, how do you think you view your chances of making it again if you were to lose it? A bit of a nuisance, right? An irritation. But a ludicrous fantasy? A crazy, impossible dream? Hardly! So do you think people with this attitude manage to make a million again if they lose it?

Yes, they do. No problem. Often they do it several times over, if they are particularly careless with money.

But when you are broke and have never managed to accumulate more than a fiddling £10,000 in small change at any one time, how do you think you view the possibility of making a million or ten million?

This appears to be an unscaleable mountain, the dizzy heights of which tower to infinity above you, a mere mortal. These slopes seem impossible to climb. You cannot imagine how another person could have climbed to that lofty peak, let alone the hundreds of thousands, possibly millions who have done so before you. There are over one million dollar millionaires in the USA alone. How hard can it be? Answer: certainly not impossible.

In your more frustrated moments you feel these people must have somehow cheated and caught a ski-lift to the top or been airlifted to the summit. Yet you know this cannot be true. A few might have sneaked to the top by subterfuge - but a million or more? Not likely.

The truth is that such a large a horde of people have tramped this path to the summit that they have left a deeply worn channel for you to follow if you care to.

Look upwards and you will see a long queue of people waiting for their turn at the peak. It's *very* crowded up there. Yet your doubt alone prevents you from following. You don't really believe you can do it.

In contrast, those who have made it and lost it know with 100% ice-cold certainty that they can make this kind of money again. They've done it once; they'll do it again if need be. It is this certainty which allows them to repeat their previous success. Sure, they have some technical knowledge and experience which comes in handy the second (or third) time around, but the real secret is their belief.

They believe they can do it. Actually, they *know* they can do it.

The poor person is filled with doubt and indecision; this prevents them from taking action. They are afraid to fail when really, they have nothing to lose.

If you're broke, what can you lose? Nothing.

Only Fear Holds You Back

Raw, naked fear takes many forms. One form is in the statement: "I don't want to be rich." Doubtless there are people for whom this is true, but I have never met such a person. I have met many people who have told me this lie, but they are exposed immediately. Most of them do the lottery!

I have yet to meet a person who would turn down a lottery win of ten million because 'they didn't want to be rich.' A more honest statement would be: "I *want* to be rich, but I'm not prepared to pay the price to become wealthy." Fair enough. At least that's coherent, and I'll be talking about paying the price in a later chapter. But "I don't want to be rich"? Come now!

So I have a question to ask you and I think at this stage of your life you owe yourself the answer:

Do You Sincerely Want to be Wealthy? One Million Plus?

It's a simple question. Think for a short while about the changes it would make to your life. Imagine winning several million pounds on the lottery. What would change? Would your life be better?

Time's up!

If you need more than five seconds to think about that one, you're in trouble! Of *course* life would be better. At the very least you would have more choices.

It would be fun, exciting, invigorating, powerful, wonderful. Forget those 'where are they now?' lottery winning misery stories slopped out for the TV viewing masses. You know, the stories about how they blew all the cash on 'toys,' got divorced, ruined the 'kiddies' and lost all their friends. Now they wish they'd never had the money. (Close up of bleached-blonde, hard-faced mum with a tear trickling down one cheek. *"We was 'appier when we 'ad nuffink. At least we 'ad each uvah. That money was a curse, that's what it woz. A curse I tell you. If I won again, I'd give it all away so help me gawd...")*

Forget all that. These stories are part of the conspiracy to keep you poor. In real life, money makes a big difference. It can't buy you health and it can't guarantee you genuine success in human relationships, and it cannot ensure happiness (that is an internal state) but it certainly improves your chances in all of these things, and the rest is yours for the asking. And by the way, in case you hadn't noticed, poverty doesn't do a lot for your health or happiness either, and lack of money has certainly destroyed millions of marriages over the years.

The 'Money Isn't Important' Fantasy

Please don't give me any excuses about 'money not being important to you.'

That's an excuse to evade the raw, naked fear which grasps your lily-livered soul whenever you think about what it might take to make some!

If money isn't important to you why are you reading a book with the title '7 Secrets of the Millionaires?'

People cling to their grim, impoverished existence out of fear, and then justify their cowardice by claiming that money 'isn't important,' that their aims are 'more spiritual' or that they would rather be poor than have all that 'hassle.'

This is often a lie.

If you have ever done the lottery or bought premium bonds then you are making a definite statement. You are saying: "I want to be rich." What other reason could you possibly have for indulging in gambling like this?

You cannot evade the answer; it is your desire to be obscenely wealthy. This desire is good, although the method is terrible!

How can you make such a strong statement ("I desire to be wealthy") and then do absolutely nothing whatsoever about it other than indulge in long-odds games of chance? It's hard to reconcile these two positions, isn't it?

The point is not to accumulate money for its own sake. Money is an enabling force. It allows you to be the real you; to go wherever you want to, to achieve whatever you desire, to actualise your dreams.

It allows a life of power as opposed to a life of quiet desperation and hopeless mediocrity. I am passionate about living a life of power. It unsettles me to see non-achievement in others - particularly those with ability.

We only have one life. This is it. Forget that afterlife and heavenly paradise stuff. If you believe this, you're dreaming. This is not a rehearsal. This is the real thing - and it's wonderful, so how can anyone squander this limited resource by trudging around the same tired-old treadmill, year after year?

The answer is - inertia.

To become rich you must change, and this means breaking the bonds of inertia. Inertia is defined as 'The inherent property of matter by which it continues in a state of rest or uniform motion.' The 'motion' being, of course, on an entirely predetermined track. To change the course of a planet or a speeding asteroid or to get a lazy donkey walking (now why did that analogy pop into my mind?) you need to apply a force. The force causes a change in direction and speed of motion.

For you, this means a life-change which will take you to new and exciting shores in the future.

What is the nature of this force which will effect a change in direction?

The Power of Your Will

It is the force of your will which does this. Inertia stifles your willpower and saps it of its strength. Hours, days weeks and even years are spent in drifting through a life divided between work, sleeping, socialising, watching TV and shopping at the supermarket. You cannot release yourself immediately from this now, today.

Why not?

Because your life has a certain inertia. Like a supertanker it cannot be diverted from its course immediately. To change course, the steering wheel must be turned by an effort of your will, and then after a few weeks or months, your life will start slowly to change for the better as it settles into its new course.

The trick is this; knowing about the time-lag between steering wheel movement and actual course change, you need to start turning the wheel early. This means as soon as possible, preferably now, today, after you have put this book down.

Now I want to ask you another question, presuming you have answered "Yes, I want to be wealthy" to the first question. It's a more difficult question:

"Are you willing to pay the price?"

I'll discuss what the price is in a moment, but first let me state that if you are not willing to pay the price you need to adjust your mindset immediately and accept the fact that you will never be wealthy, luck to one side. You should not waste any further mental energy fantasising about this, or saying "one day..." Just forget about it. Put big money out of your mind forever and be happy with what you have got.

This is a perfectly valid position to take.

You don't have to be rich. It's not mandatory. I am just asking you to stop pretending. If you've decided not to pay the price, then fine - just stop talking about it any more; it's boring. It's like saying "One day I'm going to climb Everest," and repeating this over and over for thirty years to anyone who will listen, but never taking a climbing lesson or even finding out where Everest is. Everyone around you knows this is a fantasy and will roll their eyes when you trot it out again for the fiftieth time.

One more reality check for you if you answered "no" to the paying-the-price question.

"Is it *genuinely* that you don't want to pay the price to become wealthy, or is it that you are scared?"

Think about that one for a while...

Now think about it again.

If it is just fear that is holding you back I would urge you to conquer this and push forward. Growth is everything. Fear stops you growing. Every time you overcome one of your fears, even a small one, you grow. Every time you succumb to a fear, you die a little.

Start developing a Warrior attitude. What can you lose, really? Not a lot. What can you gain? Everything you ever dreamed of. The lifestyle you always wanted. Absolute financial security, fun, power, achievement, comfort, respect, large shiny metal things with knobbly bits on the end which go 'woosh, woosh' when you wave them around above your head. *Anything*... And what's stopping you? An itsy-bitsy, pathetic little fear which you are too timid to overcome. Pah! You don't deserve a shiny metal thing with knobbly bits on the end, and I'm not lending you mine!

Paying the Price

So what is the price you have to pay? I will tell you more in chapter six, but meanwhile, here is a taster:

The price involves devoting a reasonable chunk of your life to the project of making money. Probably at least ten years, more like twenty. Obviously some have done it in less, but very few. It takes this long to learn how to do it. Actually it could take half this long if you were prepared to listen to the advice of those who have done it before you, but few are willing to do this. Anyway, it is hard to learn from the mistakes of others - we learn best from our own mistakes.

This means that you must love whatever it is you are going to be doing to make this money.

This cannot be a twenty year prison sentence. It just won't work.

You cannot mortgage your present for some future benefit twenty years down the line. You cannot do something you hate whilst persuading yourself that it will be worth it in a couple of decades when you retire. Forget it. You won't last three years, let alone twenty. That job will eat you up long before then.

To make a few million you need absolute dedication to the task at hand. This means love for your work and belief in what you're doing. If you can achieve this you'll have a great working life *and* make a ton of money. This is something worth going for, I think.

Do it Just for Fun!

This will sound strange but I believe you should have a go at making a few million just for the fun of it. People who have a one-to-one consultation with me will know that I am fond of asking: *"What other plans do you have, apart from trying your very hardest to be all you can be, to fight to dare and to win?"*

Let me ask *you* - what other plans could you possibly have that are more pressing than this? Flipping mags? Watching some more TV? Drinking down the pub? I'm anxious to hear them...

Surely there is only one plan worth having? At least it seems that way to me. The only plan a rational human being can have is to be all you are capable of being. To push the limits and keep growing until the day you die. To try for that next goal - to shoot for the bigger dream. This is a masterful life. A life filled with power. A life worth living.

But there is a price. The price is a busy life with little time for standard relaxation of the sort engaged in by the poor in pocket and in spirit. It is a 'full to bursting' life with your energies and talents directed purposefully towards positive goals. I'll have a lot to say about goals and dreams throughout this book. It is a focused life in which you work very hard on things which matter.

That's one price you will have to pay. There are others...

- You will be a driven person going from project to project.
- You will be endlessly fascinated by life and challenges.
- You will take on too much.
- Your social life will not be good because you will be unwilling to squander the endless hours it takes to maintain the dozens of friendships and acquaintances craved by the insecure. That's the truth.
- Most people will not understand you. They can't understand why you don't want to waste hundreds of hours chatting, drinking, reading tabloid newspapers and watching soap-operas.

What else?

Ah yes, I forgot to mention that almost the entire world will be against you. Most people will consider you 'lucky' to have made some money. To them, making money is a purely random event which happens accidentally 'to' someone for no effort on their part.   They spend their lives sitting around waiting for this miracle to happen to them. When it happens to you, and you get 'lucky' (after twenty years of solid effort) many people will be jealous.

You will lose a lot of friends.

8

When you become wealthy, it is just too hard for your friends to cope with because the implication is that they could do it too - and that would mean work and effort. That's bad news. They'd rather avoid you or bring you down than be faced with your silent accusation every day.

The state is against you too.

They loathe wealthy people because wealth brings personal power and individual freedom. The state detests it if a worker drone has personal power. They prefer faceless production units hovering in a no man's land of false hope, kept just above the absolute poverty line by confiscatory taxation. The burden is carefully calculated to stop just short of causing people to riot in the streets. It is designed to allow people to have some small hope of dragging themselves out of debt one day, or being able to pay the daily bills.

They do not like strong-minded, wealthy individualists. They will seek to break you down to drone status if you ever threaten to get above your station.

When people are broke, they are part of the tacit conspiracy which gives others the mandate to loot at their command. They give their silent permission because, let's face it, they are net recipients of the loot. Perhaps this was you, too? But when you have some real money, the jackboots are marching down *your* drive and it is *your* door which is being kicked in. That's a different (and non-transferable) experience.

You've got that one to come...

When you try to accumulate money, strangers will stretch out their hands and claim 'their' share of your money - and their demands are backed by legalised state violence. Resist and you will be jailed.

Your protests fall upon deaf ears.

Governments operate through the tyranny of the majority. Whatever most people clamour for, that's what is given. Anyway you're 'lucky' to be wealthy, remember? This was not caused by any action on your part. It's just a random event which happened 'to' you - or so everyone seems to think, and so it's only 'fair' that your wealth is confiscated and distributed to the needy.

All this, and more will be your lot.

Are You Still In?

Still interested? Still want to make a few million?

Good. You're my kind of person. You're prepared to fight this injustice and win or go down trying.

Are you a docile factory farm animal to be milked by the government? No. The very thought makes you angry.

Are you prepared to settle for a life of third-rate mediocrity? No. The thought makes you sick. Do you wallow in the warm human soup of vapid companionship? Do you compete with others to see who can be the more ordinary? Do you crave to be liked by all, even strangers? No? I'm very pleased to hear it.

Wouldn't it be a shame if you died not having achieved something of note? Imagine a life just like billions of others before and after you - sleeping, eating, shopping, mowing the lawn, polishing the car; until one day...you clutch your hand to your chest and slump forward head-first into the supermarket trolley. Clang!

I might be unusual. Weird even. A quick poll around ten friends and family revealed a grand total of....zero people who felt anything similar. When questioned, none of them had life-plans which were grander than the possibility of a new patio by 2005. No ambitions. No drive. No enthusiasm. Nothing. Are your friends the same?

About ten billion humans in total have lived and died on this planet since the crust became cool enough to walk on without getting burnt toes. Interestingly, that's not much more than double the number of people who are living today. That's exponentials for you - the sneaky little devils...

How many of those ten billion did anything of note during their lives? A tenth of one percent? What about the rest?

Well, incredibly they were willing to squander their irreplaceable, limited, precious life-span in dull, repetitive, mind-numbing boredom. And in many cases, this was a choice - it was not an imposition.

These faceless, nameless millions left nothing behind them apart from a new generation of the same. They are all gone now; their names forgotten. They pushed humanity forward by not one millimetre. Instead, they contented themselves with enjoying the benefits created for them by others. They were born; they consumed; they died.

Look around you. Talk to people. Do they have any burning ambitions? Any creative energy? Do they wish to leave their mark? To push humanity forward in some small way? Or are you surrounded by a new generation of grey masses who live off the talents of others? People who drive around in a machine invented by someone else - if they were to devote their entire lives to the task, they could not produce one tyre for that vehicle, let alone the complete machine - and yet they complain about how often it needs servicing. People who use telephones, TV sets, computers, videos and the like without even the vaguest of ideas about how they work, or what sweat, ingenuity and daring went into producing these miracles - all they can do is complain about Microsoft and opine that it should be stripped down to a shell and sold off for the benefit of 'the consumer.'

People who wear superb clothes when their own skills do not extend past a little crude hand-knitting, if that. People who load groaning trolleys full of top-class produce at the supermarket and moan about the 'rip-off' prices, when their own farming abilities don't run to more than a little mustard and cress and a few thin, strange-looking carrots. People who use money and banking services, who cannot even balance their own statement and yet moan about "rip-off bank profits" and complain to their MP if their bank charges them £20 for writing a letter.

Okay, not everyone has to know how to design a car or invent a new farming method, but are these people producing *equivalent* new creative goods and services themselves?

Are these people constantly amazed at the astounding array of new goods and services placed at their disposal by others? No they are not! Instead, they complain about the few percent of people who made all this possible for them - the rich, 'fat-cat' industrialists, distributors, marketers, etc. who dare to take recompense for their efforts.

Many people demand the 'right' to be allowed to consume the fruits of the industrialist's ingenuity, but they also want them broken and impoverished and their 'obscene' wealth divided up amongst the 'needy.' I mention all of this because you will be on the receiving end of this when you make some decent money. This is the nature of our society. We are ruled by third-raters on behalf of the mediocre. True ability is punished for daring to presume to be better than the lowest common denominator. The tools of punishment are draconian taxation (state theft backed by naked force) and press ridicule. Notice in the press how anyone who is not actually destitute is described as being a 'fat cat' and living in a mansion?

The Lottery of Wealth

Most people believe that wealth is a lottery, that cards were shuffled and then randomly dealt and some received an Ace, whilst others received a Two or a Three and some get the Joker. They further believe that this is just luck - like the lottery, and so those lucky people with Aces should be willing to hand over a portion of their wealth to those unlucky people with lower cards.

Closer examination reveals a different truth, and one which is unpalatable to the general public. It is not a truth they wish to hear. The truth is that with a few exceptions, the wealth creators were not dealt Aces randomly by fate. They worked at their success by making correct choices on a minute by minute, day by day basis.

Let me explain.

Everything you are and have today is the exact summation of countless thousands of little choices and decisions you made from the day you were first consciously able to make such choices. And stating it simply, those choices were mainly between action and inaction. Or putting it another way, between action and laziness. I'm not talking big, life-changing decisions here. I'm talking about tens of thousands of day by day, minute by minute choices like "shall I get up or lie in bed for another half hour?" "Should I read another chapter of that textbook or go for a beer instead?" "Should I try a little harder to get this job right, or just turn it out in a sloppy fashion?"

Thousands upon thousands of little things going right back to school days when you decided between completing a homework assignment or watching TV instead.

As Jim Rohn says, "Everything matters." It is the small choices which matter. The little day by day disciplines which build into an inexorable force propelling you towards success and wealth. After a lifetime of always choosing the easy option, the lazy way out, the least amount of work, the mediocre will have the temerity to call you 'lucky.' They will then demand 'their' share of your wealth - the wealth you built by numerous small daily disciplines, each one requiring you to forgo immediate gratification of your desires.

If anyone ever accuses you of being 'lucky' just reply: "You're right. And you know what? The harder I worked, the luckier I got."

Whilst your friends are watching soap operas or down the pub, you will be working late nights, forgoing instant pleasure, striving to create new values, new products, new ideas which will move mankind forward. Your reward? The masses will consume your products or services greedily then complain bitterly that they are substandard or a 'rip-off.' They will actively seek out minor flaws and then attempt to sue you. They will moan about how expensive your products are, demand refunds, compensation, and justice. They will support punitive taxation measures designed to extort from you the money they have paid for your products and redistribute it to the 'needy.' Blaring tabloid headlines will expose you for 'exploiting' the masses. They will demand and support tough laws and sentencing to make sure you are kept firmly in your place.

Worse...

They will say how lucky you are. How you got all the breaks and they had none. How it isn't fair. How they had that idea years ago and so the rewards really belong to them. How the 'rich are getting richer and the poor are getting poorer.' Whilst vilifying and despising the rich and successful, they will be frantically completing a lottery ticket in an attempt to join them.

Why Bother?

You might be tempted to ask "Why should I bother, faced with such a 'reward'?"

The answer is obvious. You cannot help it! The creative will always create, regardless of the odds against them, and this is the biggest weapon in the hands of the mediocre. They know that value-producers are incapable of throwing in the towel. They know that no matter how much they tax them, or ridicule them, they will still continue to produce the goods. This is why no creative industrialist (for example) ever says: *"To hell with them. I'm not paying over 70% of everything I make. I'm packing it in. I'll become a window-cleaner rather than see them get another penny."*

Apart from a few million, your real reward is nothing more than self-respect. If you get the fickle, temporary respect of the herd, then that's a bonus, but don't count on it for long!

You will look back on a lifetime of achievement whilst others recall a lifetime of drudgery. Most importantly, you will be fulfilling your true potential, and this is the greatest pleasure a man or woman can experience. The rest of humanity is content to live way below their potential, and this is the greatest misery a man or woman can experience.

So really it's a choice between a drone life amidst the poor and unfulfilled, scuffing around in poverty and misery until you sign on for celestial welfare, or a life of achievement and riches during which you enhance the world and its inhabitants rather than merely slop at the trough with the rest of humanity.

Your choice.

So how about choosing a life of power, wealth, excitement and fulfilment? How about choosing right now to have a rich and satisfying life in which you fulfil your true potential and become everything you were born to become? Why not have a shot at true wealth?

Have I got you hyped up enough to shake off that lethargy and have a shot at a meaningful life?

Great! Over the years it took me to become wealthy, I've met with and talked with dozens of millionaires - even a couple of billionaires! Naturally I've been keen to discover any common factors they share which I can pass on to those on lower rungs of the ladder.

I've identified seven common factors which I call the Seven Secrets of the Millionaires which I want to share with you in this book..

So, let us turn now to the first of these secrets.

Chapter Two
Belief in Your Right to Retain Wealth

"Believe That You Deserve to be Wealthy."

You are lost if you do not believe that having money is a good thing.

You need the self-confidence and focus to follow your dream and this will be fatally undercut if you have the wrong philosophy of life and money. No amount of effort on your part will overcome a faulty philosophy. If, deep down, you believe that wealth is a sin or that money is dirty, or wicked then the first step is for you to correct this error or give up all hopes of wealth for you and your family.

What is a 'wrong' philosophy with regard to making money?

Anything which could be described as altruistic, socialist, collectivist, communist or any one of its thousand manifestations no matter what the label, no matter what the disguise, no matter what the smokescreen.

Without exception, every self-made millionaire I have met was a rugged individualist. Most of them despised government, although many were clever enough not to say so in public. And believe me, there were approximately zero socialists amongst them. A socialist, whatever he calls himself, is someone who believes that brute force should be used to loot from the productive, in order to provide handouts for the unproductive. No matter how you disguise it, or make it look fancy, that's the plain truth of the socialist doctrine.

I believe that it is impossible for you to attempt to get rich if you have some nagging doubt that money is the root of all evil, that Capitalism is bad or that wealth should be divided up amongst the needy. You have surrendered the philosophical high ground if you sign up for any of these positions.

Let me apologise in advance if you find this section a little heavy. It is my sincere wish that you read this chapter and stay with me. Later chapters are far easier.

The teachings I produce in order to help people have a better life aren't merely plucked from the air, randomly. My views are based on a solid, 'from the ground up' philosophy of life - a thing which few people have in our compromise age of mixed economies.

It is a powerful thing to have a coherent philosophy of life. Without this, you react to life's events with a series of random, mood of the moment responses which are often contradictory and self-defeating. You pick emotions and opinions from an array of ill-considered viewpoints and hand-me-down beliefs.

In contrast, a coherent philosophy empowers you. The correct thing to do in all situations becomes obvious - it is merely a question of being strong enough to do it, which is not always so easy!

No thief, no con-man no criminal will ever come close to stealing the amount of wealth taken from you by force due to bad philosophy. I am, of course, talking about state theft of your life efforts. If you do not believe such theft is wrong, your wealth-generating efforts are doomed.

Laissez-Faire!

My desire and that of many other millionaires is simply to be left alone to create and produce.

We want our life, our liberty and the property we have slaved to accumulate. This is ours by right. These are the only real rights anyone can claim as a human being. Freedom from interference, freedom to retain the fruits of our labours and freedom from armed coercion. You should want these rights too.

All other so-called 'rights' which people march and shout for are, in actuality, the 'rights' to have others forcibly enslaved to their service.

A 'right' to jobs is a thinly disguised 'right' to have the intelligent and able thrown out of *their* jobs, by force, in order that the ill-trained, ignorant and inflexible might have jobs 'on demand,' regardless of ability.

Freedom from forced (armed) coercion is the most basic of rights. Without this, no other rights are possible. The only proper function of government is to protect citizens from forcible coercion, or enslavement, by another name.

The power of that word enslavement is not diminished by associating it with the modifier 'partial.'

A man or woman who loves freedom is not prepared to be a *partial* slave; labouring under the whip for two thirds of the year in order that they might be allowed a little sunshine and freedom in the few final months. If you love freedom, you demand freedom - total and absolute freedom. If you allow yourself to come under the lash for five minutes in a year, then you acknowledge that the principle of the whip is acceptable. Your argument then reduces merely to bargaining with the master about how much whip-free time he will grant you. Yes?

Unfortunately, you cannot become a millionaire in some distant cave hidden in the mountains - you live in a certain sort of society and the way this is run has a dramatic effect on your freedom to generate wealth. So what is the nature of this society within which you must operate?

All politicians claim to believe in the rights of citizens to follow their dream, to do the best for themselves and their family. They 'applaud' individualism. They 'acknowledge' the great contribution made by scientists and engineers, they 'encourage' greater achievement and entrepreneurship. This is what we are told by all political parties.

The reality? Well, that's different. I mentioned that the only proper function of government is to protect citizens against the use of force. Our government (*all* governments) do the exact opposite. Their prime method of operation is coercion through force and fear. This applies to everything the government does, from taxation to issuing of parking fines. You will comply or massive retaliatory force will be used against you, not, as would be proper, to protect you.

We have a 'progressive' tax system. As an aspiring millionaire you need to know and believe that few things can be more evil. Thus, contrary to government lies and evasions, the strong, fit, hardworking, intelligent, brilliant, creative people (that's *you*) are fined in direct proportion to their contribution. The cleverer you are, the larger your fine. The more creative and hardworking you are, the more of your life you will be forced to sacrifice. Struggle, kick, scream or even argue and you risk sacrificing all of your life's efforts to the agents of state control.

Where will your money go? The results of your labour? To pay for an unseen army of beggars, none of which you will ever meet. It pays their car tax, telephone bill and shopping trip. It pays for anyone, anywhere who cares to stake a claim on the fruits of your labour. You are identified as a unit of production for the state. A cash-cow. The fact that they allow you to keep a little for yourself is no compensation for the man or woman who loves freedom.

Property Rights

What about your property rights? If you aspire to millionaire status, this means that you are attempting to accumulate property and expect to retain it. What does our society have to say about your rights in this matter?

The state holds that you do not have the right to the fruits of your own labour. They have first claim on that; you get what's left. So what property rights can you have, in the face of such blatant enslavement? Why, none, of course! The state can walk right in and confiscate anything and everything you own. There are dozens of different laws allowing them to do this.

There can be no individual rights without property rights.

Next, we live in a democracy. Furthermore, this is a political system existing within a mixed economy, that is, communism in partnership with capitalism - a ludicrous and impossible contradiction. There are no guiding principles in modern politics. There is no particular direction we are heading as a country - we're just meandering around aimlessly, drifting with the tide of populist opinion. We have no goals, targets, principles, ethics or direction.

So what are politicians? Simply power-brokers. Backed by force, they extract life-values from the citizens, and then negotiate with the long queue of lobbyists who are desperate for free money. The politicians swap this free money for political power. That sums-up the current political process in our democracy.

A democracy without enshrined individual rights, is merely gang warfare - which gang, with the loudest demands can force their ideas upon the rest of us. Remember, a democracy allows 51% of the people to vote to send the other 49% to the gas chambers. Extreme, but it underlines the essential error of believing wholeheartedly in democracy as the perfect system. More realistically, democracy allows one gang to force the rest of the population to slave for them.

The statists and altruists seek absolute control of your life. The message is simple, "You are a tool of the state. We demand that you sacrifice yourself for the good of others. Your ambition, your talents your energy, they count for nothing. We will confiscate all of these and give them away so that we might retain power. Rejoice in your sacrifice."

Finally comes the exaltation, "With rights come responsibilities." Be very alert if you ever hear this.

Responsibilities to whom? Society? But since society is a collection of individuals, this becomes responsibilities to other, unknown and unspecified individuals.

What responsibilities? To feed them? To house them and clothe their children? To provide them with jobs, cars, telephones and holidays through the sweat of your brow?

You have no such responsibility and I proclaim it here and now.

If I ever do such a thing, it will be as a limited charitable gift made by me, directly to the person concerned.

"With rights come responsibilities."

What 'rights' does the statist mean? You should already have the three inalienable rights previously mentioned - the right to life, liberty and property, the latter being the right to retain the fruits of your labour. You don't need the state's permission for these rights. They are not a 'gift' of the state. They are yours with or without the *existence* of a state, let alone their permission.

So what 'rights' do the altruists mean? The 'right' to join the others at the trough? The 'right' for your share of the free money? The 'right' to be looked after, coddled and protected by a nanny state? The 'right' to have the consequences of your errors mitigated at the expense of other citizens? The 'right' to have ineptitude, idleness and lack of forethought compensated for by staking a claim in the energy and talents of others? The 'right' to waive responsibility for your own self-imposed ill-health and have others pick up the tab?

I have and desire no such rights and I proclaim it here and now.

Now I sincerely hope I did not bore you with these thoughts. The statements you have just read lie at the very core of my belief structure and are, I believe, essential if you want to make and keep great wealth.

In order to think and act like a millionaire you must have a warrior's code. A 'code of ethics' if you like, although I hesitate to use the word because it has been stolen and distorted by the very people who are trying to grab your life values.

The code of ethics for a warrior is simply one of rational selfishness.

Again, the word 'selfish' has been twisted into a spitting insult rather than a noble description of man's highest virtue. For countless centuries we have been lied to, mislead, cheated and abused by con-artists whose intent has been to trick us out of our hard-earned life-values. And they have been successful. Religions and governments have ruthlessly suppressed the people and forced them to become unwilling slaves to a higher good. There is no higher good, of course, merely the desires of the con-men for power and aggrandisement.

The concept of rational selfishness as proposed by Ayn Rand (and others) is a big subject, and one I will not try to explain here. However, if you are to become a happy, wealthy and empowered human being then you must understand the fundamentals.

How To Become Wealthy by Creating Values

Every honest man and woman should earn their own living in the free trade of values with other humans. One of the best ways to become wealthy is to create values which didn't previously exist.

Read that statement again, because it encapsulates the rational selfishness philosophy.

If you merely trade values, then you make a living but do not become wealthy and empowered. There is nothing wrong with this, of course, if that is what you want, but creativity is the key to riches.

As an example, imagine we are on an island together with ten other families. Let's trade values. I'll fix your hut roof for two hours, whilst you husk coconuts for me for two hours. Fair? Sure. No problem. Tomorrow, I'll fish for my family and your family for five hours as long as you collect firewood and water for your family and my family for five hours. Okay? Yes. No problems here. There's nothing wrong with this way of going on, and we could exist for centuries like this. In fact this is exactly how primitive societies did (and still do) operate. But there is no progress.

Why is progress desirable? Because without it we are all still working for sixteen hours a day in mindless, numbing physical toil - just as people did for centuries, just as they are still doing now in many parts of the world. The fact that we swap jobs (trade values) doesn't actually improve our lives very much apart from a slight efficiency due to division of labour.

Now, let's create some values. Assume all ten families spend three hours a day collecting fresh water from the distant mountain stream. As an 'entrepreneur' you see a way of greatly improving the physical comfort of your family whilst also greatly improving the physical comfort of every other family on the island. Indeed, you intend to *create* an honest, tradable value which will make you wealthy, but also make everyone else better off too. This is the essential point about getting wealthy through creating an honest value - everyone benefits. Note one vital principle here. You are not motivated by altruism to improve the lot of others. You are solely interested in improving your own lot, and that of your family. You are acting selfishly. How can you act in any other way? This is what gets you out of bed in the morning.

You are rational, because you know that the only sustainable way of becoming wealthy is to create something of lasting benefit to others (an honest value) otherwise they won't 'buy' it. The only alternative is for you to use force to enslave the population of the island to your desires, or to con them out of their values.

Okay, so what are you going to do? Through your ingenuity, your creativeness and your honest toil during what should be your rest period, you are going to create a neat piping system of bamboo cane which brings water down from the stream right into the village.

You plan, you scheme, you work and sweat and toil. You sacrifice your leisure and a portion of your life. You take risks - it might not work. You place yourself in danger - the mountain is steep and slippery. Of course, you need to conduct a market survey, so you gather all the villagers together and say this: *"For centuries the women have walked two miles a day to that hill with their water jars to fetch the daily water for their families. You all know that each family spends three hours a day in this pursuit. If I could bring you the same water, here, into the village and you could collect it in five minutes instead of three hours, would each family work for one hour a day on various tasks dictated for my family?"*

Now of course the resounding answer would be "Yes!" Note the vital point here: everyone is a winner. Each family gains two precious hours a day for nothing - absolutely free, for zero effort on their part. They can use this time to grow more crops, fix up the hut, or whatever else they want to do. The net effect is that their lives are enriched and their standard of living rises, all due to your ingenuity, risk, and discipline.

In return for your effort, ingenuity, skill and daring, you become a wealthy man. How? Because you now have ten families working one hour a day for you and so you can 'retire.'

In other words, because you created values for others which they willingly bought from you, you have freed yourself from the need ever to work again. There is no money on our island, but money is merely a token of so many units of human labour.

There are several important points here.

Firstly you did not force anyone to do anything. This is not slavery. The man who says that modern work is slavery is a fool who has never felt the lash on his back. In fact you freed the people from two full hours of soul-destroying donkeywork each and every day of their lives, and the price you charged them for these two hours was - zero. Secondly you did it for *you*, not for them, and you're proud to admit it. You're also proud of your water system. You're trying to add filtration and perhaps design an automatic coconut husker too. Furthermore, you are proud of your wealth and your achievements. It makes you feel good to be alive. You know you created something of lasting value, and you're receiving the rewards which you are due. These rewards spur you on to greater efforts which will make you wealthier and improve the living standard of all of the villagers.

Also, no villager is prevented from following in your footsteps, and so you act like a hero or heroine leading others on to greater efforts. Perhaps another villager will be inspired enough to start making boats in his free two hours - the two hours which you created for him and gave to him free. Now we can all go to where the fish are plentiful - by 'renting' his boats, of course. Instead of spending three hours fishing, we now spend one hour, and pay him one hour in rent. So we are all better off to the tune of another hour a day, with no drop in living standards. In other words, we work less hard for the same amount of fish and fresh water. Or, of course, we can choose to work the same hours as before and get more fish and fresh water. In other words, *everyone* has become wealthier.

How to Destroy Wealth

Note that if the island were to suddenly turn communist, the following would happen. The islanders would 'seize the means of production,' in other words, take by force that which you created and built. In this example they would seize your water system in the name of the glorious people's collective.

You would be executed or imprisoned as an 'intellectual' or 'enemy of the state.' People would be temporarily better off in the short-term because they would now have free water. Looters, thieves and parasites are always better off in the short term by stealing the values of others, but they are ultimately powerless because they depend for their existence on those of productive ability.

Incentive and entrepreneurial spirit is rapidly crushed. Your neighbour who was thinking of designing and building a boat? Forget it. He's not stupid. He saw what happened to you and so he just keeps his head down and his eyes lowered. That coconut husker never gets invented either. Society atrophies and dies. People mooch for handouts instead of engaging in creative work. The parasites and leeches suck and bleed the island dry until all that remains is an empty husk - rather like some countries I could name today!

Perhaps you are objecting that not everyone is creative and ingenious. What about the poor dull people, don't they get a break?

Yes, a level playing field is desirable. It would be nice if we all had equal chances in life, but it doesn't pan out that way. Some hunters are born stronger and faster. That's not fair, but should we weight their ankles with irons to slow them down to our speed? Pretty women get all the guys. That's not fair. Should we disfigure them to give the plainer girls a chance? Handsome rugged guys get all the girls. Should we legislate to make sure that ugly people get the same number of dates as handsome people? No, and yet society is intent upon making sure that smart, creative, bright and energetic people don't get any further financially than dull, lazy or inept people. Is this sensible and desirable? Do we really want a level playing field anyway? Don't a few hills and trenches make life an exciting challenge?

Compare the honest trade and creation of values on our hypothetical island with our current society of looters and beggars. Every penny of collected income tax now goes in handouts to people sitting at home with their palms stretched out. The rest of the governmental mechanism is funded by other taxation such as VAT, capital gains tax, excise duty, etc. Moreover, this is considered reasonable and normal. It is hardly questioned. The beggars now outnumber the active producers and so there are no votes in changing the system. The only votes to be had are in assurances to the beggars that they will get *more* free handouts, that 'fat cats' will be taxed harder and their money given away to the masses.

Since it is your stated aim to become a 'fat cat' too, you'd better have some pretty clear ideas about your own views on taxation and socialism.

Nobody, particularly a stranger, has the right to place a mortgage on your income (your life's efforts), then to sit at home whilst you sweat and strive on his behalf. But the government has made this compulsory and back this position with violence or threats of violence. You are disarmed physically (you cannot carry a gun or knife) and legally (you cannot sue the government or protest by not paying taxes). The government is the only agency allowed to use initiatory force against us. Thus, tax officers, police, VAT inspectors and hordes of others can break into your own home and drag you off to jail for one of their thousands of victimless crimes. The biggest 'crime' is not sacrificing your life's efforts to a bunch of looting beggars you'll never have the misfortune to meet.

And what is the current viewpoint of the majority of people in this country? They ridicule, lampoon and despise people who have become wealthy by honest creation of values. They seek to vilify them, scandalise them and seize their wealth. They are jealous of the talents and abilities of others so they minimise them. They focus the spotlight of the media upon successful people and wait for the tiniest slip which is then magnified. They claim that wealth earned by talent and ability is really due to luck or accident or worse.

They applaud a government which seeks to confiscate wealth and share it out amongst the beggars. They demand more free money for this, or that. They complain about the government not doing enough for them. Their lives are devoted not to the creation of honest values, but to seeking ways in which they can join the leeches, claim their share of the loot, suck on the collective tit, con or scam their share of the 'free' money.

The Plain Truth

You don't *have* to be successful and wealthy in spirit and bank-balance. You don't have to pit your wits against the world, to fight, to dare, to conquer. There are two other alternatives. You can merely trade values and barely survive, or you can become a looter and hasten the demise of yourself and society by claiming your 'share' of the free loot. But if you want a *good* life, a rich and rewarding life with material possessions and the joy of creating something which others will voluntarily pay for, then you have to act like a warrior and like the Neanderthal hunters, go and 'chase bison.'

It's honesty time now. Let me cut through the smoke and mirrors, the lies, distortions and deceit. Let us forget the altruist collectivist nonsense and be honest with each other for just a few moments. If a person sits at home moaning that the 'bison' are too far away or too difficult to catch, then what should be his/her reward, in all rational honesty? An empty larder and a hungry belly.

Start becoming rationally selfish. Think about yourself. What do *you* want? It is good, right, honest and natural to spend your life in the service of yourself and your loved-ones - although you might find this tough after being consistently lied to and conned into believing it is wicked and sinful to think of yourself and that you should sacrifice your talents and abilities to the looters.

Your alternative is to believe that every idle loafer, every single mother producing babies with no means of supporting them, the unemployed, refugees, the homeless, the feckless, criminals and scoundrels and every third-world peasant has first claim - a mortgage if you like- on your life-efforts. Only when you have fed and housed the entire queue of begging strangers can you turn your attentions to your own needs and those of your family.

The problem is that the lazy and inept now outnumber the energetic and productive. The smart producers have long ago got wind of the fact that their life's energies were being confiscated by looters at the point of a gun, and so they have disappeared, usually to foreign countries. Do you recall the 'brain drain' of the sixties? Well, it's happened, finished and gone. A lot of serious players packed up and went. They threw in the towel under the burden of supporting the 'needy,' or they faded away into more benign tax regimes.

I'm not telling you this for intellectual interest. This is not a debating society. I know how to get rich because I've done it. I've talked to dozens of others who have done the same. I want to help you get rich too. Not out of altruism, but because you're paying me.

This book has only two functions. One is to trigger your gradual awakening into the glittering world of wealth, power and personal freedom. Alternatively, it is to make you realise that you do not want this badly enough and are finally prepared to give up this particular dream once and for all.

I believe the major part of your training is for you to ruthlessly expunge any altruistic or socialistic ideas you might have. Remember, altruism doesn't mean 'being nice to people.' Altruism is the doctrine that your life is lived *for the sake of others, not for yourself.*

Let me explore this crucial idea a little further by telling you the story of two men, Rick and David.

The Story of Rick and Dave

This is the story of two friends, Rick and Dave.

Both went to the same school and came from a similar family, but early on, Rick started to hang around with the wrong sort of people at school - the losers. In class, it was Rick who made all the funny comments - everyone loved him and thought he was hilarious.

Dave did his share of playing around too, but knew exams were important and so worked a couple of evenings each week and played the rest of the time. Rick knew about the forthcoming exams too, but each time there was a choice between work and going out, he chose the easy option. He went out most nights of the week to hang out with mates, and did no work at all.

Exam day came and went, then one hot July day it was time to get the results. Dave had scored reasonable grades in seven GCSEs - not as good as he wanted, but respectable and enough to go on to take his A-levels. Rick had just three passes, two Cs and a D - the rest were fails. No chance of Rick staying on at the sixth form.

The gap between Dave and Rick had widened.

At this point in my tale, can I pause and ask you the following question? Poor old Rick has got off to a bad start in life, right?

"Should the gap between Rick and Dave be equalised, say by taking some of Dave's grades away from him and giving them to Rick?"

What do you think should be done in the name of justice?

Rick leaves school and gets a job. Actually it's quite a good job. His employer is not overly worried about Rick's lack of exam success. He knows some people aren't academic and he puts more store in enthusiasm and hard work. Rick is soon earning 'loadsamoney' and is popular down at the local pub where he'll stand a round for anyone.

He occasionally bumps into Dave who is doing his A-levels. Dave is flat broke, existing on £15 a week, but he knows that he is investing in his future. Like all investments, this one will multiply many fold and bring large returns. In contrast, Rick wears the latest designer clothes and always has a wallet full of cash, all of which has gone by the end of the month. Like most people he finds that there is always too much month left at the end of the money.

But then things start to change. Rick just can't seem to hold down a job and moves through four jobs in rapid succession. He cannot apply himself to work and just lives for the evenings when he can get to the pub - he's a key member of the darts team. Soon his CV is not looking too hot and so he starts lying about his work record and making excuses for the lack of references.

Meanwhile, Dave has graduated and started his first job. He messed around at university, like all the students, but he also worked hard when it counted - enough to get a decent degree and a good salary. The job is not much, but it's a start.

Rick is offered fewer and fewer jobs. He drifts lower down the job market, taking a cut in pay each time. He starts to get angry. Not at himself - he makes no connection between his situation in life and his actions on a daily basis - but at bosses for exploiting him and the government for not doing enough to help him. Instead of getting better, his work performance deteriorates as he concentrates mainly on the fiddles and perks which are going on at any particular company. His drinking, which was once 'a laugh' has now become excessive and a cause for concern. Everyone has noticed this, apart from Rick. Nowadays he gets aggressive when he drinks and has been involved in a few incidents. His friends all drift away as the money runs out, and then he is fired for the eighth time.

Rick signs on....

Meanwhile, Dave doesn't like his job much because it is too menial - a monkey could do it. Dave is itching for promotion.

He stays late several nights a week, unpaid, helping on a project which is not strictly in his job description. The boss notices and is impressed. Dave is going the extra mile, unasked, to invest in his future. He is doing this for *himself,* not for the boss - please take note.   A few years later, a string of well-deserved promotions have taken Dave to the top of his profession. He lives in a decent house in the best area of town. He drives a quality car and makes £60K a year. Not bad! Dave has fun with the money, but also saves 10% of it - investing for his future. Dave's motto is: "Have fun today, but invest for a better tomorrow." He's one 'lucky' guy, right?

Rick never managed to save a penny during his working years - in fact he borrowed lots of extra money to spend because his salary wasn't enough to provide for his expensive tastes. Rick stays on benefits. He sleeps in late, often not getting up until midday. He's started drinking during the day too, and spends the evenings slumped in front of the TV with a six-pack. He lives in the roughest area of town. The folk next door have a Rottweiler called Jake, on a string. It barks all night. It barks all day. Rick hates that dog - he hates the world. He's flat-broke and in debt for £18,000, spiralling out of control, heading for the deck.

The gap between Rick and Dave has widened dramatically.

Let me stop the tale and ask you this: Rick is in a very sorry state now. He hasn't got any money; can't afford a car and *needs* a better house and some new clothes. He *needs* a wallet full of cash.

Should Dave be forced to give half of everything he earns to Rick in order to close the gap between them? Let me continue the story...

Dave's ex-girlfriend Judy has done rather well for herself too.

For the last ten years she has worked 100+ hours each week to build her vegan restaurant into a thriving success. At one time she had every single penny of her money invested in this enterprise and had borrowed £60,000 from the bank to finance it. She worked, sweated and toiled at that restaurant through the long evenings whilst Janice (Rick's ex-girlfriend) was clubbing with her mates.

Janice works at the local Safeway as a check-out girl. At five o'clock on the dot she's out of there.

She has been passed over for the supervisor's job many times. She doesn't want the 'hassle' and besides, each week on a Thursday there are supervisors' meetings which go on until *six o'clock*, unpaid! No chance! Thursday is a good night down at the club.

Janice lives in a bedsit and can barely live on the £125 a week which her 'skinflint' boss pays her. She thinks she is worth at least double that figure, but can't say exactly why. However, she is very clear on the fact that she *needs* at least double her salary.

The gap between Janice and Judy has widened considerably since they were at school together. It's not fair, is it? How come Judy gets all the luck?

Do you think we should take half of Judy's restaurant revenues and give them to poor Janice? After all, she *needs* the money, right?

Recently the government made a statement concerning the 'obscene gap' between the rich and the poor in this country. Not only was there a *gap* (horrified gasp from party supporters) but...the gap was actually *widening*! The government then vowed to do everything within their power to address this terrible situation and to close the gap as quickly as possible.

In this one statement you see the full horror of the government's philosophy. This is an undisguised, full-frontal attack on inventiveness, ability, hard work, discipline and commitment - the very qualities you are going to need if you want to become wealthy.

What is the clear message behind a stated desire to reduce the gap between rich and poor? It is the standard collectivist or communist ideal of breaking everyone down to the lowest common denominator.

Instead of taking the best of mankind and hailing them as a shining example of success and achievement, to be emulated by all, they take the worst, the lowest, the biggest failures, the weakest in spirit and the most morally bankrupt. These are the people who are elevated to the position of importance.

And how is this 'gap closing' to be achieved? In the only way open to governments - through brute force. Money will be collected from the productive (Dave and Judy) under threat of violence and handed out to the 'needy' (Rick and Janice) in a variety of ways. If Dave and Judy protest, they will be arrested, imprisoned and their money confiscated anyway.

The unstated principle is this: *"Disciplined hard work will be penalised progressively - the harder you work, the greater the proportion of your efforts we will confiscate. The poorer you are, regardless of the reasons for that poverty, the more money you will be entitled to as a right."*

If a gap between rich and poor is seen as a huge social evil, to be eradicated at all costs, then surely there is no tolerable limit to the size of that gap? In other words, the unstated aim must be to reduce the gap to zero, otherwise the claim is nonsense. It would be ludicrous to state something like: *"We are aiming for a society in which the richest person is no more than 14.34% wealthier than the poorest person."* Why? From what moral basis is this statement made? If 14.34% why not 25% or 100% or 500%? There is no answer from the government because they are not arguing from defendable principles but from vote-grabbing expediency.

The Effect on Dave and Judy

Now what is the effect on Dave and Judy when they see well over 50% of everything they earn being confiscated and handed to Rick and Janice?

Dave becomes depressed. He just can't seem to do much better than he is. He has reached a plateau from which superhuman extra effort is required to bring him marginal rewards. He is angry at the government and sometimes feels violent. He's starting to understand why people march in the streets and overthrow despotic regimes. But he's law-abiding and so pays his taxes. He becomes a depressed sheep in the government's pen. Nothing can stop his creative spirit and productivity though (governments know this - it's impossible for a man or woman of ability to go on strike unless you break them completely) and so he keeps producing, like a dutiful little soldier, for the government coffers.

Judy is more feisty. She puts two fingers up at the government and decides to cheat on her taxes. She keeps two sets of books and has offshore accounts through which she channels a certain proportion of her takings. The government have turned her into a criminal. Her crime is to attempt to retain that which she worked to achieve - one of the biggest crimes you can commit in the eyes of any government.

The efforts she would have put into expanding her restaurant business into a chain of restaurants are now diverted into criminal activities such as cooking the books instead of the lunches. She is too preoccupied to notice four suited customers who seem a bit out of place in a vegan restaurant. They prod moodily at their plates of brown rice and vegetables and seem more interested in the other customers. In fact they are part of the government's multi-billion pound enforcement Gestapo. They are counting the customers and takings with the aim of trapping her.

Next week there's a tax raid with five officers bursting into the premises. Diners scatter in fear and Judy is taken into a back room for questioning. Yes, she's guilty of the horrendous crime of attempting to keep her own money. She is prosecuted and demands are issued for an arbitrary and fictitious sum totalling twenty times the amount she siphoned off. Judy sells the restaurant but even that is not enough to satisfy their insatiable demands. She gives them every penny she owns - the results of ten years of long, hard labour. They still want more. She declares bankruptcy. This is exactly the result they want - another 'smart ass' jumped-up woman put firmly in her place. Judy never starts another business. In fact she draws state benefit for the rest of her life.

Why am I telling you this story in a book on how to become a millionaire? Because unless you understand the way your country works, you cannot have the moral strength to have a contrary opinion. Without the moral strength - the belief that what you are doing is good - you will have a hard time succeeding.

Understand that 'gap-closing' means taxation. Taxation means the creation of a vast army of bureaucrats costing hundreds of millions in confiscated loot. It means a huge Gestapo with unbridled powers of search, seizure and arrest. It means doors kicked-in, prosecutions, bankruptcies, broken people, destroyed businesses and lives. It turns productive people into compliant wimps or worse, it perverts their basic honest tendencies and corrupts them. It forces them to become criminals in order to survive.

The Effect on Janice and Rick

But what is the effect of all this on Janice and Rick?

They are net recipients of the extorted loot. The government use the money stolen from Judy and Dave in order to buy the votes of Janice and Rick. They get more free loot - not a lot, but then there are millions of other 'needy' people and only a few like Dave and Judy to produce it.

Do you think this acts as an incentive for Janice and Rick to improve their lives? To get up out of the chair and start working? Or do you think they take the money and then carry on exactly as before? Does Rick feel guilty about taking this unearned, stolen money, or does he think he deserves it - that it is his 'right'?

I maintain that it is not desirable to 'close the gap' between rich and poor.

Why not? For the same reasons that I would not give half of Judy's restaurant to Janice because she 'needs' it; neither would I transfer half of Dave's GCSE results to 'poor old' Rick. This should be plainly obvious to anyone.

A gap between rich and poor is not only good it is an absolute indicator that we are still alive and twitching. The removal of such a gap would imply a totalitarian Big Brother state in which homogeneity was the noblest ideal and mediocrity the goal of every man and woman.

Closing the gap implies redistribution of wealth.

Whenever you see the phrase 'redistribution of wealth' be very alert. It smuggles in a hidden premise.

At the base of this statement lies the proposition that nobody really knows who created the wealth; that somehow we all 'chipped in' our little bit - we don't know exactly how - to form a great communal soup of wealth belonging to all. It then becomes the government's duty to redistribute this wealth by ladling it out fairly starting with the most needy. But this is an evasion. We know that wealth is not produced in this way and to pretend that it is, requires the anaesthetising of your rational mind. This is what I mean by evasion - the wilful turning away from the facts of reality in order to support a wish.

Wealth is created only by men and women who apply their rational minds to the facts of reality. The greatest of these women and men, the true heroes and heroines of our country, create incalculable benefits (wealth) for everyone by gearing-up the efforts of the ordinary person, just like in our island water-system example.

If a man chooses only to earn a living by coarse muscle power alone, then the ingenuity of the wealth producers allows him to gear-up his muscle power a thousand-fold by using a machine. Even a spade is a simple machine, thought of by somebody, designed by somebody. Without it, the exponents of brute muscle-power would be scrabbling at the dirt with their bare hands.

Your rationality is your prime tool of survival. Other animals survive using speed, cunning, brute strength, teeth, claws, stealth, disguise and a whole array of other techniques. Man cannot survive using the methods of other animals. Why? Because like other animals, man has his own unique essential nature. He is a rational animal and his rationality is his prime tool of survival, without which he would literally starve to death.

The extent to which a person applies their rational mind to the facts of reality, is the extent to which they become wealthy - call it surviving and prospering if you prefer. The extent to which you evade reality, subscribe to fantasy, illusion, religion, emotionalism, mysticism or resort to the brute methods of a savage is the extent to which you are powerless, trapped, poor and helpless. And this is a choice you make, daily, hourly.

The way you think society should be run is likely to be an exact reflection of the extent to which you believe people should be protected from their own idleness or ineptitude.

Put another way, to what extent should people be buffered from the consequences of their own choices not to conform to reality? Should they be compensated and even rewarded for their active decisions to embrace mysticism, illusion or inertia and laziness?

This would mean that one person's *need* is all that is required to create an automatic mortgage on another person's life - that person is just a sacrificial animal, to labour for the needs of others.

What would be the clear, unequivocal message?

Work hard, apply your rationality to the problems of nature, create wealth, become independent of the state and you will be attacked, looted and penalised to the maximum ability of the state under threat of imprisonment. Sit back, be idle, write a list of your 'needs,' issue your 'demands,' make no provision in surplus times for the lean times, save nothing, spend everything, do not look after yourself and the state will smile upon you. You will be excused from all of your obligations regarding your welfare, your health and your children's education. This will all be paid for by the productive.

Of course I want to make one vital point which I hope I hardly need to make. You may support any and every case of poverty or hardship you come across, at your discretion, by voluntarily donating up to 100% of everything you own - but not a penny more. For the record, I help several such people in this manner.

The Rights of Man

To conclude this more difficult philosophical portion of the book, let me ask you what are the inalienable rights of man?

Briefly, they are life, liberty and property.

The pursuit of happiness is really an aspect of liberty and so does not need stating except for one very important point. It describes the *reason* why man requires liberty. The specific reason stated is the pursuit of happiness. That is, a person's own goals, his or her own life. It is a statement that man lives for his own sake, not for the sake of others. This was a very profound recognition by the founding fathers of America.

Without 'the pursuit of happiness' it could be argued that yes, man needs to have life - that's obvious; yes, he needs freedom - nobody would deny that. Why? So that he may more easily engage in altruism and sacrifice to others of course!

Now the rights of life, liberty and property were not just plucked out of the air - a set of floating demands. Firstly notice what they all have in common.

They place no demands on others. They do not insist that others sacrifice themselves to satisfy your rights.

Ultimately they are little more than injunctions to be *left alone*. If I were ever asked by the government what they could do to improve my life, I would unhesitatingly say: "Please, please, *please* just leave me alone. Get out of my life, get your tentacles out of my business, get your prying eyes, your spies, your enforcers, your bureaucrats and your monitoring systems off my case. Stop looting me, stop regulating me, stop interfering with me."

These three rights also have one other important thing in common.

All three things (life, liberty and property) are nothing more than a statement of the fundamental requirements for a man's survival, as man. They reduce to the following statement: *"I need my rational mind in order to survive as a man. My alternative is to survive as an animal, or half-man, half-animal. I have a right to survive as a man, using my essential, given nature."*

The fundamental right is the right to use your rational mind which is your primary tool of survival. It is your right to survive, not just physically, like a brain-dead vegetable, but as person, and it is *this* right which statists will attack by any means at their disposal.

An attack on any one of the three basic rights is an attack on your right to exist as a man or woman, through using your rational mind.

Life

Removal of your life is the ultimate act of destruction against your rational mind. After death, no further action is possible.

Liberty

You must be free in order to exercise your rational mind. If force is used against you, then you are immobilised until the force is removed. Partial force immobilises you partially, making you less than human. If you are imprisoned, restrained or your life-efforts looted then your rational mind is constricted down to a smaller version of what it might be.

Property

The product of your rational mind is wealth. If you are not allowed to keep your own property, then the efforts of your mind become pointless. There is little point in allowing Einstein his life and his liberty but confiscating and burning each page of his notes as he completes them. No rational person can operate like this because in order to survive, man's goals must be long-range. Unlike an animal, he cannot survive from meal to meal. Long-range goals imply freedom of thought and action. They imply the accumulation of property, possessions and money to act as a buffer against life and to fulfil man's primary directive - to be happy for himself, for his own reasons, for his own ends.

There are several important things about rights - real rights, as described above.

1. You either have rights or you don't.

Philosophically, there can be no watered-down half measure in which sometimes you are allowed your rights, but at other times you are not; such occasions to be determined by government whim. Either you believe that man has a right to exist as man, or you believe he is a worker ant in a socialist colony to be used and disposed of by the current masters. You are either a *free* man, or a slave. Being whipped by the master only on alternate Tuesdays, does not make you a free man.

2. The function of the government is to protect individual rights. That should be its only function.

The word 'individual' means one solitary man or woman. Therefore, in such a society (which we do not have) there can be no such thing as 'group rights,' 'Aboriginal rights,' 'women's rights,' 'gay rights' or 'ethnic minority rights.' These would be redundant terms. If *every* individual's rights are protected, you have no need of group rights. What more could they achieve? It would be like saying: "All people have a right to eat the food of their choice" and then having achieved this right, starting a movement demanding that lesbians be given the right to eat the food of their choice too. This is already covered by the concept of individual rights.

Most 'group rights' activists are either campaigning for the basic human rights listed above (in which case they should be campaigning on behalf of *all* men and women) or they are screaming for the unearned - the extortion of loot, favours, values or special treatment from one section of the population to be given to the campaigning minority. Most often it is some sort of crazy, mixed-up mess containing both.

3. Because force is the most basic way of violating rights, **any civilised society renounces the use of individual force**, and hands this power (the ability *to initiate* force) over to a dispassionate government. This power - the power of destruction - should be there solely to protect the rights of individuals. Any government that uses this force to harry, cajole, intimidate and oppress individuals is a force for pure evil. They are beyond mere evil if they use this weapon to destroy man's basic rights by, say:

1. Looting property through force without recompense.
2. Arbitrarily passing laws to limit man's reasonable pursuit of happiness.
3. Restricting liberty by passing thousands of victimless laws.

So it will come as no surprise to you to learn that the government is your deadliest enemy in your pursuit of wealth. No bandit, no robber no hoodlum will ever inflict one thousandth of the damage on your wealth which the government will inflict upon you.

You will not change the system. That is not the point of this discussion. The point is that you need to recognise the anti-life, anti-business, anti-wealth society you inhabit and then to discover your own internal set of principles which allow you to carry on the struggle. You must hold a firm moral belief in your own goodness.

Without such a belief, you will be crippled by the current destructive philosophy which surrounds you. You cannot hope to escape this philosophy - the philosophy of altruism - because it is everywhere. Every news article, every TV programme every film you watch will espouse one or other version of this. Your only hope is to recognise it for what it is, and then to hold the contrary opinion firmly in your mind, if not in public.

Most importantly, if you sign up for any version of socialism in your mind, then you are a dead person, financially. Your beliefs will undercut your wealth-creating efforts. In effect you will be engaged in an activity which secretly you despise and think is evil on some level. This cannot continue and you will find yourself sabotaging your own efforts. I have seen this so many times.

You need to decide, right now, what your philosophical position is.

To succeed, you need to be right up the Laissez-faire Capitalism end of the spectrum and as far away as possible from the Communist end.

Having disposed of philosophy, let us now turn our attention to the remaining six secrets.

Chapter Three
It All Starts With a Dream

"If You Don't Have a Dream, How Are You Going to Make Your Dreams Come True?"

It all starts with a dream...

Let me tell you up front that if you do not have a dream, you will not become a millionaire other than by winning a game of chance. It's just too hard.

To make this kind of money you need to be laser-beam focused, and you can't be that if you only have a half-hearted interest in what you are doing. You know this is true.

How? Just look at some famous multimillionaires who still keep working ten or twelve hours a day, even though they don't need the money.

Why do they do this? Because they have a passion for what they do. They would probably do it without payment!

Dreaming is a type of visualisation. It is visualisation plus passion. These are the things that you *really* want to be, to have or to do. If you do not achieve these things over (say) the next ten years, you are going to be seriously disillusioned and upset.

You should be able to write a list of six such things. If you cannot think of a single one then you are most unlikely ever to live a life of power and passion. Also, your chances of making big money are vanishingly small. If you like, this is your first reality check.

Can you think of a few things about which you are passionate? One or two things which you care deeply about? Just one would be a start.

Don't beat yourself up if you cannot immediately think of something. It is hard to dream up a better life for yourself due to the decades of negative conditioning you have allowed yourself to accept. How often did your teachers, parents and friends encourage you to dream and ask you to share your vision with them? Approximately never? I thought so! How often did someone shoot your fledgling dreams down in flames or pour scorn upon them? Small wonder that your dreams are not on public display.

The Future You

Here is a little exercise which might help.

Imagine walking into a room and meeting the 'you' of ten years from now. What will you be wearing? Where will you be living? What will your lifestyle be like? What car will you be driving? Will you be running a business? If so, how successful will you be? What will your net worth be?

You really only have three choices here about how the 'you of the future' will look, and this is where the power of this exercise lies:

1. Somewhere in between how you are now, and a depressed, broke and scruffy tramp.
2. An exact clone of how you are now - absolutely nothing has changed in a decade.
3. A happier, wealthier, healthier version of the 'you of today.'

Only a suicidal depressive would visualise number one. Number two is effectively saying that nothing will change; you will not grow over the next ten years, you will not get richer, happier, wiser, healthier - anything. The 'you of tomorrow' will be indistinguishable from the 'you of today.'

So that just leaves number three, and if you selected this it remains for you to back this glittering vision of the 'future you' with all the force of your imagination.

Having imagined how you will be in the next ten years, here is a really neat to trick to help you achieve it.

Ask yourself the following questions:

☒ "What do I need to achieve in the next <u>12 months</u> in order to make my future dream a reality?"
☒ "What do I need to do in the next <u>month</u> to start myself on this journey?"
☒ "What can I do by <u>next week</u> to prepare myself for the journey?"
☒ "What can I do <u>right now, today</u>, in order to start this process off?"

Do you see how this works?

You need to dream, but this is not enough. Dreams come a size too large so that you can grow into them and this means that dreams are too large to realise all at once.

Our minds are finite, and so all large projects must be broken down into bite-sized chunks otherwise we become discouraged by the scale of the endeavour. This is one of the secret keys of successful people. They are undaunted by large projects, because they have the knack of breaking them down into simple steps. Each step is easily manageable, and can be completed in anything from a few hours to a few weeks.

In contrast, it is useful to analyse the situation of people who are stuck, both monetarily and in spirit, if only to allow you to avoid these errors. This is based on my experience of two decades of dealing with both winners and temporary losers in the game of life.

1. They are frightened. Their lives are dominated by fear. They see the world as a scary, threatening place and crave security, dullness, mediocrity. They long for every day to be the same as the last and become scared and upset if even a small change breaks the monotony of their days.

2. They completely lack visualisation ability. If asked to visualise their future self, they would stare at you blankly. *They are not pretending.* They do not even understand what you mean by this exercise. If you force them to try, they'll come back with nothing more than a shrug.

3. Assuming that you could drag some sort of dream out of them (for example wanting to be worth a million pounds some day) then they would be wholly incapable of working backwards from that point to the present, and suggesting actions they might have to take in order to make this come about. Again, *they are not faking*. There is now; there is the future; and in between, a yawning, fathomless chasm - a blank.

4. Even if you were to write the steps out, 1-100, with a check box next to each one, they absolutely lack the discipline even to start on the task, let alone complete the steps. At the first slight downfall, or negative comment from a friend, they will give up. In any situation which requires a choice between working for a better future, and instant gratification now, they will unfailingly choose instant gratification.

But this is not you, hopefully. If you recognise yourself here, then don't worry because it is possible to change and get out of this 'stuck' pattern you are in.

You need to develop the habits of a winner. You want to enjoy today, but have an even better tomorrow waiting for you. To do this you must model yourself on winners - people who have achieved great things in their lives. I am talking here about 'winners' and 'losers' but I do not mean the term 'loser' in the usual derogatory sense. By a 'loser' I mean someone who, by their own definition of winning and losing, is falling well short of where they want to be. By a 'winner' I mean someone who, by their own definition of winning and losing, is pulling ahead of the game and achieving that which they set out to achieve.

This is how a winner operates:

1. They are brave. Like all human beings they feel fear, but have mastered it and are able to rise above it. Whilst they acknowledge that there are frightening people and places in the world, in general they view the world as a benevolent place, full of great opportunities and wonderful people. This is a vital principle. Winners view the world as mainly benevolent with some bad bits. Losers see the world as mainly malevolent with some good bits.

2. They are good visualisers. They have the ability to imagine the future, often in glorious Technicolor detail. They have high self-esteem, and know that they are worth more than they have at present. Life to them is an exciting adventure to be lived to the full. In contrast, losers view life as a terrible chore to be somehow 'got through' with as little pain as possible.

3. They are intelligent, rational and logical. If they have a dream of the future, they know the secret technique for making this happen. Today's dreams are tomorrow's realities. They know that large projects cannot be tackled by finite human minds unless they are broken down into manageable, bite-sized pieces. They are able to work backwards from a future dream to the present day, and to list the logical steps required to make that dream come true.

4. Having written down the steps required to achieve their goals, they know what is required next. **Action.** Up until this point, all of their plans amount to little more than ethereal hot air. It is *action* which grounds the circuit and allows the current to flow. They know that the journey will be long and hard. Any worthwhile dream will involve hard work, concentrated effort and some suffering to attain. They need one more quality. Discipline. This keeps them going during setbacks, when the list seems too long, and when others heap mirth and derision upon their efforts.

Five Tips to Turbo-Charge Your Dream

1. Dream of a brighter tomorrow. Your yearning power is more important than your earning power.
2. Be rational. Mysticism is your mortal enemy. There are obvious, logical steps between here and your dreams. Write them down in bite-sized chunks and follow them like a route map.
3. Act. All is dust without action. Action is the key.
4. Be disciplined. Life is tough. Fight. Others want you to fail. Ignore them. The world is against you - go your own way. People will spout rubbish - ignore it.
5. Start today. Procrastination is the thief of time. Winners start right now. Losers chatter to themselves that they will start 'one day real soon.' It never happens.

Hierarchy of Needs

All dreams are driven by your needs. This might be your need for approval, recognition, status, safety, love, food, shelter - or any one of a hundred different needs. So when thinking about your dreams, I want you to remember this concept called the hierarchy of needs - you might have come across this before. It goes like this:

When life is a desperate struggle, we are overwhelmingly consumed with the desire for food. Every waking moment is spent in pursuit of nourishment. Nothing else matters. We scrabble the earth from dawn until dusk with little on our mind apart from the thrill of discovering another root or berry. There is little time for philosophy or self fulfilment. We work, we sleep, we eat - if we're lucky.

Food is the first need, assuming we have basics such as air and water. If, due to man's ingenuity, we manage to crack the food supply problem, our next need becomes shelter and warmth - somewhere cosy to lay our heads at night. If we achieve all of these things, the next thing we seek is love and belongingness.

And after that?

Recognition, self-esteem and the esteem of our peers.

This is a very important realisation for you. It is very likely that you already have air, water, sufficient food, a roof over your head, a modest amount of money, and a certain amount of love and friendship. Therefore your dreams will almost certainly reflect your next need on the list which is your desire for recognition, self-esteem, admiration, respect, fame, achievement, etc.

If you want ten million pounds, then this is almost certainly because you want to *be* somebody and have the respect and admiration of society, not because you need a larger roof over your head or extra food.

As an interesting aside, the modern phenomenon of the serial killer coincides exactly with a period when, for the first time in history, most people have adequate food, shelter and warmth. Next in the hierarchy of needs comes love, which we will assume is thwarted for some reason. So the next higher need is recognition. Or, in the case of the criminal, notoriety. Most serial killers when caught and questioned, mentioned that one motivating factor was the desire to *be* somebody - a rare motive in crimes from previous centuries. Paul John Knowles who embarked upon a random killing spree in 1972, claiming the lives of at least 24 victims, declared himself to be "the only successful member of my family" and positively basked in the media attention after his arrest. He was subsequently shot dead by an FBI agent whilst trying to grab a gun after a court appearance.

Recognising your desire for adulation, fame, infamy - call it what you will - helps to clear your head and focus your mind more firmly on your goals. It can also help you to detect erroneous or incorrect dreams. Yes, there are such things as incorrect dreams. I would define this as a dream which is an overly complex or grandiose strategy for filling a simple need, when a far simpler (and more achievable) strategy might suffice.

Achieving a net worth of ten million pounds is actually a difficult task and one which will exercise you for the next ten or twenty years. There is absolutely nothing wrong with this, if it is what you really desire. But if this dream is being driven by a craving for recognition, admiration or respect then there may be an easier way of satisfying your desires without going through the twenty years of grief required to amass ten million. Perhaps you can get the recognition you crave in some other simpler way by writing a book, appearing on television, being a star in your local community or any one of a hundred easier ways. It's just something for you to think about.

Once you understand that it is our need for recognition, not money, which drives most people in an affluent Western society, you will be less puzzled by the things that are going on around you. The rise in crime and delinquency is not caused by poverty, it is caused by tens of thousands of petty crooks wanting to 'be somebody,' or 'teach society a lesson' or to 'get respect' - they are, if you like, ego crimes not fiscal crimes.

A century ago most crime was survival crime. People stole to eat. Vandalism was almost unknown. A vandal leaves his or her mark on the furniture of society - it is a statement of ego.

The dramatic rise in divorce rate has little to do with people being worse husbands or wives these days, compared with the past. If anything, they are a lot better. It is driven by people's desire for recognition. They want to be appreciated. They are not prepared to suffer the drudgery of marriage without reward. A century ago this would have been unthinkable. You got on with it because the survival of your family was at stake. Your precious thoughts of wanting appreciation were inconsequential in the scrabble for plain survival.

Look at advertising on television. Most products are sold on the basis of raising your self-esteem, not on the benefits of the product. Most adverts these days have the hidden message 'be somebody.'

So learn to look at your dreams with a critical eye. Ask yourself what the underlying need is behind the dream and then ask yourself if this is the only way you can achieve it. Don't get fixated on the actual method or strategy of getting the need met; often there are many different ways of achieving satisfaction. First work out what the actual need is, and then plan the simplest, most realistic strategy for meeting it.

Many people struggle throughout their lives to make big money only to find that when they have got it, they still feel hollow and empty. This is because the money was just a symbol for the underlying need - which still hasn't been met. A classic case would be a woman who sacrifices everything to reach the top of her profession and make a lot of money, only to realise that she has spent twenty years trying to gain her father's approval and love and this was the way she thought she could get it! What a hard route - and it didn't work! If only she had recognised the underlying need (for approval and love) and considered some alternative strategies, any one of which could have been far easier than the struggle she put herself through.

How To Discover Your Dream

I would like to recommend an excellent book which will help you to discover your hidden dreams - those you have locked away since childhood and dismissed as 'impractical.'

The book is called *"I Could Do Anything if Only I Knew What it Was"* by Barbara Sher. Isn't that a great title? It is published by Dell Trade (nothing to do with the computer company) and the ISBN number is 0-440-50500-3.

This book seems to come in and out of print, so you might need to find a second-hand copy. She has written several similar books, all of which are worth reading. My copy came from Waterstones priced £7.99.

As the title suggests, *"I Could Do Anything"* is a book about life-planning. I have read several books on this subject over the years, and to be honest, most are a bit of a yawn. Although they contain a few nuggets of useful information, and the odd pointer to a better, brighter life, they are usually dull and uninspiring. They also tend to contain tedious exercises such as this:

"Take a sheet of A4 paper, and down the left-hand side list 37 emotions ranging from apathy to anger. Now down the right-hand side of the paper, write about 37 episodes in your life when you were feeling each of these emotions. Recall your experience in vivid detail. Remember what you were doing and who you were with."

Sure...right... I'll do that when I've got the odd spare week and the attic doesn't need clearing out or the drains degreasing... In contrast, Barbara's book contains only a handful of exercises, all of which are quick and easy to do.

There is one exercise, which I will share with you in this chapter, which is quite simply the most powerful life planning exercise I have ever come across. Completing this exercise will cause a profound change in your life, and will give you an amazing insight into exactly what you should be doing. This probably is not what you are doing now.

But first, let me pause for a moment and say something which is, admittedly, not very cheerful.

I believe that most people are suffering from low level depression. Take a look around you. How many people do you know who are genuinely happy and fulfilled? Don't get me wrong, I am not saying that most people are terminally depressed or suicidal. People get by. They cope. Life jogs on. But I think you will agree that few people are motivated, passionate and happy.

Statistics back up what I am saying. Over five million people in the UK take antidepressants daily in order to cope. That's a stunning figure.

So what is the cause of all this unhappiness? Surely not money. The rich and poor alike queue at the prescription counter of the local chemist. I can tell you as a straight fact that money does not guarantee happiness. Money merely gives you choices.

Let me tell you what I think is one of the largest contributory causes. It is the fact that people are not following their own personal dream. Worse, most people do not have the faintest inkling of what that dream might be, or even that such a dream might exist. Like so many rusty, disused railway wagons they were shunted off the main line many years ago and now find themselves standing in some remote siding, far away from the clear, straight lines used by express trains, and with innumerable points and crossovers lying between them and their intended track.

Let's face facts, most people are living somebody else's life, not their own. The shunting operations started early, usually at school.

Most schools have a slick statement in their brochure which goes something like this: *"We at xyz school believe that each child is an individual. We believe in nurturing that precious individuality so that the child may fully express their own unique talents and inclinations."*

The reality is this: *"We at xyz school, believe in a regime of reducing any smart-arse individualist kids down to the lowest common denominator by using our time-proven methods of ridicule, fear and punishment. We undertake to eradicate each child's uniqueness, and we pride ourselves in turning out a uniform batch of worker drones to fill the labour market."*

Does that sound more like the school you attended? It certainly sounds like the one I went to.

So, that unique, special, quirky person which is the long forgotten you, was shunted off the main line into your first side-track.

Side-tracked

You probably had the glimmer of a dream when you were a youngster, but this was soon knocked out of you. Your parents undoubtedly called your dream unrealistic. Then, to the sound of a points-lever being pulled, they suggested to you that you get a 'practical' education in order that you might follow your dream at a later date. I am not implying any malevolence here, you need to remember that your parents, and all preceding generations did not have the luxury of fancy life-planning.

The name of their game was survival. To survive you needed money. To get money you needed a good job. To get a good job you needed a good education. They pulled those levers on you for the best of intentions, but the result was a disaster for your fledgling ambitions.

This message was reinforced by teachers, friends and careers advisers, until by the time you left full-time education you were almost certainly way off the main line and heading fast down some insignificant branch line.

Throughout these years, you learned the trick of suppressing your dream. You simply could not maintain this dream in the face of such ordered opposition and so you buried it in a secret place within you.

Then the pace of life started really to heat up, and problems started to come at you like a pack of hungry jackals. No time for fancy, childish dreams now. All of your energies were involved, and probably still are involved, in fighting off the pack of slavering dogs. Dreams are... well, for dreamers. There is a life to be lived, food to put on the table, a mortgage to be paid and other people to worry about.

If you even remember your dream, you probably fool yourself into thinking you'll pick it up later, when the family has grown up, when you are retired. Some time. The tragedy here is that most people's dreams become so deeply buried they not only forget what they are, but even forget that they had a dream in the first place. Certainly, few people can put a name to their dream. Instead, they sit in the sidings, rusting away, perhaps (if this is not pushing the railway analogy too far) hoping that some bright, gleaming locomotive will arrive one day to pull them to safety.

Is it any wonder that they are depressed?

I want to make another important observation at this point.

To be fair, I do not think that we are well equipped to get in contact with our dreams and to plan a glittering, fulfilling and exciting life for ourselves. Man has only existed for around one million years, perhaps two million at the absolute maximum. For 99.9% of that time, we lived short, brutish lives which were wholly obsessed with creating sufficient food, water and shelter for our basic survival. Few people lived beyond 35 years old. I strongly suspect that life-planning was not an issue which occupied the thoughts of men and women prior to a few hundred years ago.

Even the wealthy had few choices. The son of a rich family joined the army, became a priest, or took over the running of the family business. In general, he was not full of angst regarding his special purpose on the planet. Such thinking is a luxury, brought about by material wealth and the increase in health and hygiene. We live longer. We are all richer. We have the luxury of being able to consider our true purpose and we have the leisure time to be unhappy if we do not fulfil that purpose.

Living a Meaningful Life

I believe that each person is a very special, unique individual.

I also believe that everyone has a passion - if only they could discover it.

And let me state one final belief: I believe that if you will only follow your passion - your dream - then everything will be all right. It will work out. You'll make enough money to live on, perhaps even get rich, but more importantly you'll have a joy-filled and truly meaningful life. The alternative is to live a life like our primitive ancestors - gruelling, desperate, toil-filled days devoid of meaning other than brute survival.

The difference is that they had no choice. You do.

Now I want to say a word about 'meaningful.'

Do you, like me, equate the words 'meaningful' and 'dream' with something hugely important; of tremendous significance to mankind? For example, do you think that a dream in order to be meaningful has to be something like this?:

☒ Invent antigravity.
☒ Invent faster than light travel.
☒ Write a book which will profoundly change the lives of all six billion people on the planet.
☒ Create a world-changing philosophy.
☒ Eradicate poverty, disease and hunger from the world.
☒ Overthrow the government, and start an entirely new political system invented by you.
☒ Write a series of symphonies which make Mahler and Mozart look like amateurs.
☒ Climb every mountain; ford every stream; follow every rainbow.

In other words, are you trapped, like I was, by the belief that your 'meaningful dreams' have to be grandiose, or they are not worth pursuing? Do you believe that small dreams are for small people and that only giant dreams are worth having?

If so, what on earth are we to make of dreams like this?

"I was a cost control accountant for IBM. One day, two years ago, I was driving through the countryside on my way to a sales meeting. Suddenly, about half a mile away, I saw a broken down windmill. To this day, I don't know what happened, but something about that windmill called to me. As though guided by a will other than my own, I turned off the road and drove down the bumpy track leading to the mill. It was completely deserted, and dilapidated. Using my mobile telephone, I cancelled my meeting. I don't know what possessed me. I had never cancelled a meeting before except for serious reasons such as ill health. Little was I to know that this was the most important cancellation of them all. At that moment I knew I wanted to own that mill and restore it to full working order. Of course, it was crazy. I had a responsible job, paying a good salary. I knew nothing about windmills. Literally nothing. Correction: I knew that they went round and round, and somehow ground corn into flour. But at that moment I found my passion in life. To cut a long and difficult story short (for I will not pretend it was easy), I located the owner of the mill and purchased it from him. I gave up my job and career and moved with my family into a house near the mill. We spent two years restoring it, and now run it as a working windmill and museum. I'll never get rich running the mill, but we make enough to make ends meet. The important thing is that the last two years have been the happiest of my life. Perhaps I won't always own the mill. It's possible I might get tired of it one day. But that doesn't matter. By then I'll have another dream and I will know that it is possible to follow your dreams and to succeed. From where I am sitting, I cannot even begin to understand how I spent so many years as an accountant. It seems utterly fantastic to me now."

This man is not going to save the world, cure all known diseases, or eradicate poverty. He found a dream which was his unique destiny or vision, and had the guts to follow it. His dream was entirely insignificant on a global, or even local scale. He did not change anybody's life apart from his own.

What were the needs which this dream fulfilled?

I can only guess. Perhaps he needed to create something with his bare hands. Perhaps he needed to control something in its entirety - be responsible for all of the cogs, rather than just be a cog himself. Perhaps he wanted to earn his living in an honest way, and saw accountancy as basically a dishonest profession. Only he could tell you.

No Approval Required

It is *your* dream that counts, not somebody else's definition of what constitutes a valid dream.

You do not need to get your dream countersigned by society and have them approve it as big enough or important enough. The dream is for *you,* not society. It matters not one jot if a single other human being benefits or not from your passion. You're doing it because you want to do it. That's the only reason you need. If you want to make money from your dream, then it will have to benefit others as well, but it's a very rare dream which has no positive impact on the lives of others.

Big, planet-changing dreams are allowed, of course! Just make sure it really *is* your passion, and not something you are claiming to believe in for one of these three erroneous reasons:

1. It's so big you know you'll never do it, and so there's no point in making a start. In other words, your grandiose passion is little more than an excuse for inaction.

2. This is not really your passion, but you think it sounds grand enough, altruistic enough, or worthy enough to be allowed under society's definition of 'meaningful.' in other words, you feel that small, personal dreams are not allowable, are too insignificant and make you look like a loser.

3. Your dream is merely one, grandiose strategy for filling your need - you could fill that need far more easily than via this complex and unlikely scheme you have envisaged.

When you get in contact with your passion, and follow it, remarkable life-changing events will happen to you - sometimes not exactly what you might expect. Here is a story taken from Barbara's book which illustrates this point well.

The Story of Jessie

Jessie was 45, very quiet and shy. She lived in Atlanta, Georgia, and ran an office for her husband, a well-known architect. He was a star in his community, involved with meetings and parties while Jessie did all the unglamorous paperwork.

Jessie had no idea what she wanted do with her life. She joined a six person Success Team (a self-help group of about six people who meet regularly to make each other's dreams come true). Jessie's team did everything they could to help her find something she'd love, though she couldn't come up with a thing.

"Why don't you look for a job you like better?" They asked. *"I don't know,"* she said. *"I just don't feel like it."*

Months went by. Then one day, Jessie walked into the group and announced: *"I want to race sled dogs in the winter race at Bear Grease."* (Bear Grease is a small town in Minnesota.)

The team was flabbergasted.

"Are you sure?"

"Yes," Jessie said. *"That's what I want to do."*

"Do you mind telling us why?" They asked.

"I don't know why," she said.

"Do you know anything about sled dog racing?"

"Nope."

That was the end of the team's questioning.

Before I go any further, see if you can guess at the need which this challenge might fulfil in Jessie.

Her team were so happy Jesse had found something she wanted that they set out immediately to help find a training school, or a dog racer, or anything. They approached anyone walking any kind of dog and asked, *"Do you know anything about sled dog racing?"* Finally, somebody did know about a summer training camp for dog racers, and on a warm summer day, Jessie walked into camp, went up to the trainer, and said, *"I want to learn how to run the sled dogs."*

He looked at her, a tiny 45 year-old lady in a straight skirt and sensible shoes, and decided to discourage her. He hitched up the team of dogs to a training sled on wheels and gave her the reins.

"Here," he said. *"Practice a little. See if you like it."*

Suddenly he shouted to the dogs and they took off running. Jessie could barely keep up with them. She tripped and slid and practically fell on her face, but she stayed with the dogs all the way around the track.

When she finished and caught her breath, she smiled at the trainer and said, *"I love this!"* He laughed, and consented to train her.

When winter came and it was time to go to Bear Grease, Jessie realised she knew nobody. She asked her trainer if she could use his name for introductions and he said, *"I can't do that, Jessie. You are still a beginner, and I have a reputation to maintain."* So Jessie's Success Team took her to the airport and saw her off with loud cheers and secret fears.

When she arrived at Bear Grease she found a tiny town, mostly one main street, packed with snow and full of seasoned sledders sitting around in clumps with their dogs. She forced herself to walk up to one crew after another, asking if anyone needed a helper, until finally, someone who had lost an assistant to the flu took her on. And Jessie ran with a team of sled dogs over a hundred mile course.

The Success Team went wild when she called after the race and when Jessie returned home, she was a satisfied woman. She told her team all the gripping details with a big smile on her face. *"Now, that's happiness,"* one said. *"It sure it is,"* Jessie said. "*What now?*" her team said. *"More training?"*

"No," she said. *"I'm finished. I don't want to do that any more."*

There was a moment of stunned silence and then her team said, *"Well, what do you want to do now?"* Jessie said, *"Quit my job."*

It had never occurred to anyone in Jessie's team that she would need to overcome a big challenge before she'd be ready to give up her thankless job and go out into the world.

That was an excellent example of the power of dreams. Jessie knew she wanted to change her life, but could not summon up the courage to quit her job outright. She needed this intermediary dream to help her realise a bigger goal - that of independence. It was, if you like, a 'steppingstone' dream.

Your Job From Heaven

I now want to share with you an amazingly powerful method of helping you to realise what your dream might be. I am indebted to Barbara Sher for this idea.

Before I explain this exercise, I want to give you an example of a technique which has some merit, but is not very effective. This is the sort of technique you'll read about in books on life-planning, and I find it very unsatisfactory.

Take a sheet of A4 paper (yes, you can start groaning). On the top of the paper write the words 'My Job From Heaven.' Underneath this, write out exactly what the title implies. This is fantasy time, so let your imagination run riot. You can design your own perfect fantasy job. Where will you work? Who will you work with? In what sort of environment? Doing what? What hours will you work? What salary will you be paid? Is it a manual job? A creative job? Just put down anything you can think of which would make your working day blissful.

What do you think of that for an exercise?

Okay, it has its merits, but if you actually try to complete this exercise you'll find it fairly difficult.

The reason is that the second you try to fantasise about your ideal job, negative thoughts and conditioning crowd your mind, effectively saying to you: "Don't be silly! You can't have that! That would be impossible. That's asking too much."

Now, and I hope you're ready for this...take another blank sheet of paper and on the top of it write: 'My Job From Hell.'

I want you to fill that sheet of paper with a detailed description of your total job from hell. Describe the nightmarish work environment, write in detail about the crummy people you'll be working with, and the awful tasks you'll be performing. I can guarantee that you will hardly be able to stop writing. You will take a ghoulish glee in putting down every awful detail. You'll run out of paper and ink long before you run out of ghastly details of that job.

This exercise gives you a fantastic opportunity to glimpse your creative potential when you are not running hard against the brakes of the subconscious mind.

Please do this exercise, and don't only read about it. You'll be quite stunned by its effect.

The next part of this exercise is to take your Job From Hell and write the *exact opposite* of everything you have put down.

For example if you have written "I work in a dark, noisy, fume-filled factory, with loud pop music blaring all day over speakers," you need to rewrite this as follows: "I work in a light, quiet airy office." Another example should suffice. If you wrote "Each day is identical to the last, I produce an endless stream of identical widgets, and never receive any praise or thanks for my work," you need to rewrite this as follows: "Each day I work on something different, no two projects are the same and I receive a huge amount of praise, admiration and respect for my work."

Get the idea?

What you are doing is using the 'Job From Hell' as a method of bypassing the subconscious mind. Effectively, you are finding out what you *don't* want, and reversing it to produce your Job From Heaven.

When I sat down and used this technique, I was quite surprised by the results. I found out things about myself which I had not been aware of before.

Reading through my completed Job From Heaven (produced by reversing my Job From Hell) I felt a thrill of excitement running through me. Yes, this was *exactly* what I wanted to be doing.

Try it yourself - you will be surprised!

The Fear of Finding Your Dream

Another extremely powerful technique is as follows:

Finding your dream is a very scary process. Suddenly, there are no more excuses. You are faced squarely with the terrifying knowledge that you have a passion and that you long to follow it. The next step is, of course, action. But most people are petrified by fear when faced with the decision to change their lives dramatically. Our IBM accountant hinted that this was not an easy process for him.

I should mention that one of the reasons we keep our passions submerged is because we know that once we 'release the beast' we will never be the same again, and our comfortable, boring routine will be upset. Big change is frightening. It causes tension and anxiety.

Through many years of lecturing and training people in life planning, Barbara Sher has encountered this problem over and over again, and so she has devised a technique for overcoming this obstacle.

What you must do is:

1. Vow to take action towards realising your dream, *right now*. But...

2. You only have to do this for *one hour*.

In fact, Barbara insists that you set your alarm clock for one hour from now, and then spend the next sixty minutes - not a minute longer - in active pursuit of your dream.

Example: Assuming the IBM accountant had not taken immediate action, he would follow this system by setting his alarm, and then spending sixty minutes doing the following type of actions:

1. Telephoning the owners of working windmills and talking to them about the benefits/pitfalls of owning one.
2. Trying to locate the owner of the mill he saw.
3. Doing an Internet search on Windmills and trying to find if there was any useful information for the aspiring owner.
4. Ordering books on windmills from Amazon.com, etc.

Jessie would have, in that hour:

1. Called every friend she knew with a dog and asked if they knew anything about husky racing.
2. Done an Internet search on husky racing and Bear Grease.
3. Called the local RSPCA and asked if anyone knew anything about huskies. Etc.

I think this is a brilliant technique. It gets you moving towards your goal and totally overcomes the fear and pain associated with starting out on a huge life-change. It also programmes your subconscious mind that you are *serious* about this change. It isn't just talk.

Another thing I can throw in the pot at this point is the old adage: "When the decisions are clear, the way is easy."

Fight Your Fear!

So much of your life-energy is wasted in endless debate, procrastination, agonising and worry about the effects of your decisions. If you would only take bold, decisive action, then something almost magical happens. The way opens up for you and the problems and obstructions melt away. I'm not claiming that the transition will be silk-smooth, but I can promise you that half of your fears will be unfounded, and many of your anticipated problems simply will not happen.

What's really going on is subconscious resistance to change. We really do fear change, for good survival reasons. But in order for you to have a joyous, sparkling life, you need to embrace change and welcome it into your life.

Consider the 'you' of today. Forgive me, but I bet it's a pretty dull routine without much excitement, right? Also, do you have any real plans, or are you just jogging along, letting life happen to you? I also bet you're in a job which you tolerate, but *certainly* has nothing whatsoever to do with that quirky, brilliant 'you' inside. Remember? The one which got suppressed all those years ago?

Start trying to uncover that buried desire - and don't let 'shoulds' and 'oughts' get in your way!

Try, just for once, to listen to yourself without immediately leaping in with habitual negative thoughts about the impossibility or impracticability of your dreams. Even if your dream seems crazy, at the very least it will point you in the right direction and perhaps trigger a more realistic dream.

Remember, the purpose of a dream is to get a deep need filled in you - the dream is just a vehicle or method for getting your needs met. So when I ask the question "what are your dreams?" I am really asking you "What are your needs?" It is your needs which have been suppressed all these years, mainly by thoughts of sacrificing your needs to the needs of others.

So what better time than right now to examine what it is you really need, what it is you are *really* on the planet for? Out of countless thousands of generations of humans, you have the sheer luxury of being born into a time and place where you can decide how to live and what to do. That's scary, but also amazingly exciting, don't you think?

Chapter Four
You Must Have a Plan

"To Make Serious Money, You Must Know What You Want and Have a Plan for Achieving it."

There is a well-known yet powerful method of achieving everything you want in life. It only takes five minutes. Anyone can do it but hardly anyone does. Imagine - something you can do in just five minutes which can send your income through the roof, improve your relationships and power-boost your life towards total success. Wouldn't you want to do that right away?

I'm talking about the time-honoured technique of goal-setting.

It has been proved beyond reasonable doubt that people who set written goals lead richer, happier, more fulfilling lives than people who merely drift through life, rudderless.

Now if you're yawning and thinking "seen it, done it" I challenge you to go right this moment and fetch your own list of goals. If you are able to do this, it marks you out as very special. If you cannot go and get your goal list, right this second, may I suggest you stifle that yawn and take a few minutes to do this exercise?

The great motivator Brian Tracy is fond of recounting how often people come up to him and say something like this: "Brian, a year ago I attended your seminar and you got us to do that goal exercise. Well, I did it, but only because you said so. When I got home, I put that piece of paper in a drawer and forgot about it completely. I found it a couple of weeks ago and you know what? Six out of ten of those goals had been achieved by me without my even remembering I had set them!"

Now since this is so easy why do so few people do it?

Why People Don't Write Goals

For a person wilfully to miss out on the staggering advantages of setting goals, there must be a psychological block somewhere. I believe the block is the subconscious realisation that every goal has an associated price tag - that it doesn't come free. It doesn't "flow freely from the wondrous bounty of the universe." There is a *price to pay* in order to achieve each goal. This knowledge evokes fear which triggers inertia and this stops you from taking this important first step.

Of course most people realise this subconsciously, and after a decade of research, I now believe that I have isolated the main reason why people do not set goals.

It is not ignorance. Everybody now knows the importance of setting goals. Thirty years ago, this was a startling new idea. No longer. Goal setting is a powerful and proven tool for success in any field of endeavour. Everybody knows this, but still they don't do it.

Why?

It can't be the difficulty of the task. Writing out ten goals is not a particularly arduous job - in fact it is quite enjoyable and only takes about twenty minutes. And yet 98% of people never write a goal in their entire lives, even though the task of writing out your goals is so easy and the rewards so obvious.

It isn't even the difficulty of pondering what it is you ultimately want out of life - just ease yourself in with some simple goals, say to move up to the next biggest house and to earn an extra ten thousand pounds this year. Leave complex life-goals ("Who am I? What's it all about? Why am I here?") until you are happier with the whole goal-setting process.

No, there must be something else, and I think I have identified it.

To set yourself a goal means to set yourself up for change. Any goal that you can think of, large or small, basically reduces to the statement: "I hereby promise to change in the following way..." We all fear change - it is the unknown. Fear stops us dead in our tracks.

Above everything else, a goal is a written contract with yourself to *do* something. To achieve even the smallest goal requires discipline, work, and focus; all three in some measure.

How do you think people react when faced with a contract containing the words 'discipline,' 'work' and 'focus'? Why, they break out into a cold sweat. Their hands tremble and seem unable to grasp the pen. They go to sign, then draw back, then go to sign again. Suddenly, they feel faint. The pen slips from their numbed hand and clatters to the floor. They'll sign that contract one-day real soon now - perhaps tomorrow...

I believe this is why people don't set goals.

Something For Nothing

The people who do not set goals still want all of the rewards and goodies which *would* have come their way had they set goals and applied the discipline, work and focus. They want all of these things, but they want them for free. They seek to short circuit reality, and this attitude leaves them vulnerable to the happy-clappy, "you can have it all" seminar snake-oil artist.

The packaging varies, but the message is essentially the same: "The universe has an infinite store of wealth, bounty and benevolence - there is more than enough for all. Just tune your mind into the pulsating rhythm of the universe using the following method (tape set £49.95, book £29.95, course £199.70) and claim your share of this infinite bounty."

People love this message. They sign up for it in their millions in one form or another. They think: *"Why bother to sign that stuffy old contract with all those tedious 'work, discipline and focus' clauses? I could have it all for free merely by tuning in to the bounty of the universe!"*

And so a few more irreplaceable years slip by. They buy the books; their collection of boxed tape-sets grows. Yet strangely, they remain as broke and powerless as ever. How odd! Seems like the 'mystic bounty of the universe show' is on 104.3MHz FM, and their brain is tuned to BBC Radio 4 - long wave! *"Hmm - perhaps another seminar will help me re-tune my cosmic receiver..."*

I cannot resist telling you a little true story which illustrates this perfectly. A couple of years ago I wrote a booklet entitled "How to Double Your Way to a Million Pounds Starting From Nothing." You've probably seen this, but basically it's a bit of fun with a serious message. The first step is to find a penny in the street. Then, you go through a process of just 28 steps, doubling your money each time, 2p, 4p, 8p, 16p and so on.

Surprisingly, if you were able to do this just 28 times, you would end up with well over one million pounds! I take out adverts in the press which describe this system and offers my booklet for free. It really is free, and you don't even pay the postage to send me your request because we use Freepost. Recently we had a customer on the telephone shouting and raving. He was going to take us to Trading Standards. He was going to get a crowd of mates together and personally pay us a visit. He called us a bunch of conning b***s and he was going to get us, whatever it took. The reason? He had received my free booklet (which cost him not one single penny) and he had had it for one week but still not received a million pounds from out of thin air.

This man, who seemed sane by the way, was virtually incoherent with rage; he was screaming and swearing, shouting and threatening. I thought this was an extremely good example of the *hopeless irrationality* exhibited by many people.

So if you do nothing else, please deprogram yourself from the erroneous belief that goodies will 'flow' to you if you only concentrate hard enough. That's not how our universe works and authors who produce books and tapes implying that this is so, are doing people a great disservice.

Writing a few goals is not a difficult exercise - each one only takes a few moments - but the point is you actually have to *do* the exercise in order to receive the benefits**.** Simply reading the exercises is not enough.

The rewards of life come to those who *do*, not to those who merely read, talk or day dream. Action is the key.

Now, with your permission, I would like to ask you a simple question: *"Thinking back over the last twelve months, did you achieve all you set out to achieve?"*

This is a 'yes or no' answer, so don't spend too long considering it.

The answer, of course, is 'no' - unless you are a pathological liar!

Next question: *"Did you set out to achieve anything in that period?"*

Aha! Now that's a more interesting question I think.

Deciding at the start of a year that you want to achieve a certain result by the end of that year, is another example of goal-setting.

High-performance people set goals. Winners set goals. Losers never set goals. Why? Because it takes about twenty minutes of concentrated effort to write down your goals, and people have far more important things to do than this. It interferes with valuable drinking and socialising time, for example. Such a task would take up nearly a whole episode of a soap opera. You could read a tabloid newspaper from cover to cover in this time.

But there is a more important reason why many people don't write goals as I have intimated already. Writing goals commits you to action, otherwise there is little point in writing them.

Turning your dreams (goals) into reality will not happen automatically. It will require work and effort.

"Ohmygod! WORK, and EFFORT? Forget it! I'm not writing down anything on a piece of paper which will commit me to that!"

This is why people do not set goals (write down their dreams). They cannot bear to have that piece of paper leering at them in silent accusation as the months and years tick by.

But what is at stake here? Nothing less than a solvent, even wealthy, lifestyle, improved happiness, and a fulfilled life.

Perhaps more importantly, you can meet your fear head on and live like a warrior, not a frightened rabbit.

Why Are We All So Afraid?

The older I get the more I wonder what it is we're all so afraid of. Like you, I travel the world and see or hear about *real* problems; murder, torture, death, disease and starvation. Then I return to this grey, stuffy country to witness intelligent and privileged people wasting their lives down the pub or propped in front of the TV screen for, on average, four hours each night.

Many people are also timid and completely risk-averse. Their quest for safety comes way above their desire for pushing the boundaries and living a powerful life.

Achieving great wealth and happiness starts with having a dream. Today's dreams are surely tomorrow's realities.

No matter how far down you are at the moment, I promise that you can make a greater success of your life from here on in. Not only have I done this myself but in the past ten years I have helped thousands of people to improve their lives. These are people similar to you. People who were sick of the poverty and mediocrity of their lives, just like I was twenty years ago when a small book changed my life forever.

It's a famous book called: **The Lazy Man's Way To Riches** by Joe Karbo. Cheesy title and Joe is long dead, but that was the very first exposure I ever had to the ideas of positive thinking, motivation and goal-setting.

The book was sold mail-order at £10. Like millions of people I thought: "Yeah, I know how *he* got rich - by taking £10 off mugs like me!" To this day, I receive about one hundred letters each year which say the same thing about the advert for my own book **The Midas Method.**

Anyway, I thought "what the heck" and decided to give it a shot. (Note: Investing in myself). To my surprise, the book arrived and I remember the thrill with which I opened it. The book was dynamite! It talked about goal-setting and motivation. I had never heard such concepts. It talked about the magic power of goal setting and how it worked. I was highly sceptical, but decided to try (Note: You need flexibility. You must be willing to try something different, even if you 'know' it's rubbish.)

I set my first six goals. One of which was to have a net worth of £250,000 one day. Note this goal. At the time (and I can recall it vividly) this was an impossible, fantasy level of money and I didn't believe for one microsecond that I would ever achieve this. I was about £20,000 in debt on a salary of £6,000/year. But the book said to set high goals, so I chose a 'ludicrous' amount of money. (Note: False ceilings keep your aspirations low. What a *low* goal to set, whilst thinking it was an impossibly *high* goal!)

Something changed that day. Imperceptibly. No flashing lights and blaring trumpets. Just a small shift in gear and a tiny angle-change in aiming point. I was not even aware of the change, but looking back I can say categorically that writing my first set of goals was the turning point. If I had not done that, I am totally convinced that I would have remained a studio engineer at the BBC, or similar.

Instead, I decided to fight. Are *you* prepared to fight?

Writing Your Goals

Within the next hour, you are going to get out of the chair and write yourself a fistful of goals. Here's how:

On a single side of plain, A4 paper, write a list of ten things you would like to achieve in your life; five long term, five short term.

The first goal should be something which you cannot complete in your lifetime. This makes you think carefully. It makes you realise what is important to you, and why you are here. The long-range goals stop you being frustrated by short-term setbacks.

You might be very surprised at what you write for this goal - it might have nothing to do with your present life.

As an example, if you are a writer, your goal might read: "One day, every educated adult on the planet will have heard the name Stuart Goldsmith, and have some idea about his philosophy." By the way, that isn't one of my goals because I am not out to save the world - just *you*, you miserable sinner! But it is a good example of something that would transcend my lifetime.

The next goal should state an exact amount of money which you will one day have. Again, this is a lifetime goal and should not carry a date. Example: "One day I will have a net worth of ten million pounds." This goal quantifies your dreams of wealth and sets an ultimate target. But before you write this particular goal, spend a few moments considering if you are willing to pay the price. Don't want to pay the price? - then don't write such a grand goal. I'll discuss more about paying the price in a later chapter.

After you have finished writing your list, I want you to look at your 'money' goal and answer the question: "What one thing can I do right now, today, which will take me a step closer to this goal?" It could be a simple thing like a telephone call, but write it down as your eleventh goal: "By the end of today I will have................. which will advance me one step closer to my financial dream."

The rest of the sheet is for eight specific time-dated goals. For example: "By January 1st 2003, I will have moved into a four-bedroom, detached house in large grounds."

Goal-Setting Tip #1

Do not get bogged down in worrying about if goals should be in the past tense or future tense; or if they should be written at midnight or midday. The bottom line is that none of this matters nearly as much as actually writing them!

Goal-Setting Tip #2

Do not write a goal in the hope that you will attain it by mystical methods; that somehow the 'bountiful universe' will cause this money to 'flow' to you. It won't. That stuff is for dreamers. To make your goals come true requires action on your part.

Goal-Setting Tip #3

Buy yourself one of those natty little credit card wallets at some point in the near future. They are small leather wallets with individual clear plastic pockets designed to hold about ten credit cards. Write out your goals onto credit-card sized pieces of white card. You should keep the cards in this wallet and carry them with you always.

Normally, goals are written on a sheet of paper - fine if you live alone; you can leave it lying around to remind you of your goals. But if you have a family, or people coming to visit you regularly, then you don't want these people to see your private dreams. So what happens is that you put the piece of paper away in the drawer - and there it stays for several months! I really like this card idea because it means that you always have your goals with you, and they remain private.

Goal-Setting Tip #4

Before writing a big life-goal, do a double check to see if you can uncover the underlying need. It would be a great shame to spend your life pursuing a grandiose long-term goal when in reality this just stands as a symbol for an underlying need - a need which could perhaps be filled far more easily.

How Many Goals?

Remember: Ten things only.

I could have made this a list of fifty or even a hundred items, but this would take an hour or so to complete, and I know from experience that this would result in most people not even starting the job. So, <u>ten things only</u>.

Could I suggest that some of the items are fairly major projects? I would like to make a further suggestion. These projects should take you a little further down the path of where you want to be in life.

As an example, imagine that you have always fantasised about being a rich and famous author. A suitable goal might be: "Complete outline and first chapter of novel."

Compare this with a task which would probably take longer to achieve, but would not move you one inch closer to your life's dream, e.g. "Completely re-landscape garden and plant ornamental trees and shrubs." Although a useful job, unless your aim in life is to become a renowned landscape gardener, I think you will agree that this task does not move you closer to where you want to be in life.

Here's another example. Let us assume that you have always wanted to become a millionaire "one day," and that you fancy your chances in direct mail publishing. One of your goals might read: "Spend one day coming up with ten exciting mail-order business ideas, write each idea down on half a sheet of A4 paper, and rate them 1-10."

Now that goal will move you closer to your dreams of becoming wealthy, whereas this goal does not: "Take a week off work and spend it reading up on Greek mythology." Assuming, of course, that this is an interest of yours. Notice that this goal also consumes seven days instead of one but does not advance you closer to your dreams. The point here is that if you are only going to set ten goals, then make some of them goals which will move you toward your dreams, as we discussed in the last chapter.

But what are your dreams?

Before you can successfully write goals, you need to have a dream. You cannot make your dreams come true if you don't have any dreams! This sounds obvious, but only a tiny percentage of people can name their dreams: one, two, three on request - and these are the people who will eventually achieve them.

I have deliberately presented this important topic of goal-setting in reverse order to make you think about it.

Effectively I have asked: *"Did you achieve your goals last year?"* Followed by: *"Did you <u>set</u> any goals last year?"* Then I suggested that you set ten life-changing goals and finally I asked you to consider your dreams in order that you might successfully select these goals.

The Key to Success

Now the correct order (the key to success if you like) is as follows:

1. Dream.
2. Break your dreams down into bite-sized chunks.
3. Set weekly, monthly, yearly goals which move you inexorably closer to your dreams.

I'm talking here about big life-planning goals. There is a very real place for smaller goals of the 'trim the hedge, paint the workshop, read up on Roman history' variety, but these goals are not the topic of this book. We're talking here about the secrets of the millionaires - the entrepreneurs who have made their fortunes.

As Robert L Schwartz so aptly stated: *"The entrepreneur is essentially a visualiser and an actualiser... He can visualise something, and when he visualises it he sees exactly how to make it happen."*

Your big dreams and projects are just too complicated to keep in your mind and retain as a coherent whole. If you do not break your dream down into achievable steps, it will remain exactly that - a dream - a fantasy which you keep repeating but never take any action to make it happen.

If you consider the dream "Land a man on the moon by 1969 and return him safely to earth" then I think you will immediately see the impossibility of this project taken as a unit. Only by breaking it down into ten different subsections (propulsion, human safety, navigation, communications, etc.) and then further dividing each section down into ten or more other subsections can you hope to get any kind of grasp or control over the project. Your dreams might not be quite so ambitious as a moon shot, but nevertheless you still need to break them into bite-sized chunks if you are to have any hope of succeeding.

I remember one man who came to me for a consultation recently. His burning ambition was to own the largest collection of old British fairground rides in the country - a strange dream, but this was his passion. His eyes took on a sort of Holy Glow when he started talking about Dodge 'Ems from the 1960s and carrousels from the 1940s.

I hope you can see that this dream requires immediate breaking down into several steps. Off the top of my head, these steps might be:

1. Finance - these rides are expensive, how is he going to raise the money? Loans? Sponsorship?
2. Location - the rides are huge, and if you own a hundred of them, you might need an acre or more, under cover, of course! Where should he locate the museum? How will he pay for the ongoing expenses?
3. Preservation - what do you do with the rides when you own them?
4. Commercial exploitation - is there a buck to be made here? Quite likely. If he has a passion for old fairground rides you can bet that others do as well, and will pay for the privilege of visiting a working museum.
5. Planning Laws, etc. - what are the safety implications or environmental implications?

I am sure there are other areas that need considering. Each of the above five steps can be further subdivided into five or more mini-steps, and perhaps further subdivided again. The trick here is to move from an 'impossible' and nebulous dream to a series of actionable statements such as "Make appointment to see Bank Manager," or "Telephone English Heritage and make an appointment to discuss the feasibility of this project with them."

One Small Step For a Man...

Do you see how this works? Land a man on the moon? Own three million pound's worth of antique rides? Forget it! Those are impossible dreams to hold in your mind together with all of their ramifications. But 'make a telephone call' or 'talk to chief scientist about feasibility' - these are readily achievable.

How do you reach your dreams? One small step at a time. How do you make a fortune? One pound at a time, that's how!

Thinking about the fairground rides for a moment, this is a good case for examining what the *real need* is behind the dream. Owning fairground rides is not a need - it is a strategy for filling a need. Is there a better strategy? I spent some time with this man examining his real needs and together we worked out that he could fill his need (for admiration and respect) a little easier than this fairground plan.   The purpose here is not to puncture dreams - it is to maximise your need-fulfilment in the simplest possible way. Being humorous for the moment, you don't want to spend thirty years of your life amassing fairground equipment if this is driven by the fact that your Dad refused to take you to the fair once, when you were seven. This wasn't the motivation of my client, by the way!

If it turns out that your dream is the best and most exciting way for you to fill your needs, and you are passionate about your dream, then go for it and don't let a single person stand in your way. Set goals to help you achieve your dream. Make some goals large and some small. Your large goals act like beacons, guiding you onwards in the right direction, but they contain no detail; this you obtain by the process of breaking each goal down into achievable steps.

Take Ten Minutes to Change Your Life Beyond all Recognition

If you have not started to write your goals <u>within ten minutes</u> of reading this chapter, then it is almost certain that you will never write a goal in your life. The consequences of this are too awful to contemplate. You will live your life at about one tenth of your ability and potential. That would be a terrible waste of your talent.

Do not let this happen to you when such a simple exercise can change your life forever.

I implore you to write your goals, now, before you move on to chapter five.

I'll leave the final words with Jim Rohn:

"Goals. There's no telling what you can do when you get inspired by them. There's no telling what you can do when you believe in them. There's no telling what you can do when you act upon them."

Chapter Five
You Need Discipline

"Successful People Know That They Must Sacrifice Something Today in Order to Achieve a Lot More Tomorrow."

For years I denied to myself that this was one of the secrets of becoming a millionaire, or achieving anything else of note for that matter.

I think the reason that I avoided naming this secret was because I dislike the word 'discipline.' There's something Dickensian about it - more than a whiff of the workhouse and shades of 'honest toil for the bosses,' but there isn't a better single word which adequately covers this concept. 'Focused Will' is close, but that's two words. Single words work better for concepts like these, so we're stuck with discipline.

In my discussions with other multimillionaires, this was the word they used most frequently when trying to explain their success. I became really excited when I finally accepted this. A lot of things fell into place. This was the *key concept* which differentiated the rich from the poor; the successful from the failures.

Discipline.

Without it, you're one of the 80%+ - the failures in life. Remember, this is not my judgement on others - I have no right to judge. These people are failures by their own admission and definitions. If you were to ask them if they feel they have succeeded in life, or failed, they would readily confess to having failed, although they would, of course, blame factors outside of themselves for this failure.

With discipline, you have a good chance of rising above the crowd and retiring early as a wealthy man or woman.

Everything I write is aimed at preventing you from reaching retirement with nothing. If you reach retirement as a pauper dependant upon charity, having lived a life of quiet desperation, frustrated, never having achieved anything much of note, not really having had a good time (apart from the odd high point), never having dreamed, never beaten a real challenge, then your life is a failure *by any standards*, but certainly by your own. Of course, if you are happy in your powerlessness and poverty, then none of this matters.

Are you a disciplined person, in general?

There are hundreds of indicators of a disciplined mind, not one of which is essential, but put together, they start to add up to a pattern. Can you get up in the morning? Are your shoes clean, your hair and teeth brushed? Are your car and house tidy? Are your personal papers (gas bills, bank statements, etc.) filed in some sort of reasonable order? Do you turn out a good job of work, even when nobody is looking? Do you ever get drunk? (No disciplined person would *ever* get drunk!). Do you use recreational drugs? I could think of five hundred more indicators, but you get the idea. It's up to you to look at your life and make an honest assessment of your level of discipline or lack of it. Again, I am not judging you. Live how you want to live, including in a pigsty, unwashed and doped-up half the time - it's your life. But if you want a life of power and wealth, then I can guarantee you will not get it if your life is anything like I have described.

Discipline is vital.

When I meet consultation clients face to face, I often say something like this: *"There's nothing really special about me. I'm just an electronics engineer made good. You could do what I have done."* I say this to try and remove the 'guru factor.' You can't get people to emulate you if they think you're the incarnation of a sun-god! So I tell them I'm just a regular guy, and that's the truth. Yes, I have an education and a certain amount of common-sense. But I also have discipline. Often, the people sitting opposite me do not have discipline, or at least they haven't made it central to their lives because, heck, it takes discipline to be disciplined! I can see the lack of discipline in the way they dress, the way they sit, and the way they talk.

What is Discipline?

Well, I guess one definition is being strict with yourself.

You know why discipline is important for a child or teenager, don't you? It's to keep them in line. It's to stop them getting out of hand - getting away with too much. Also, you discipline your children out of love, and not because you enjoy the power-trip (I hope!). Often, you *hate* to discipline your kids because it spoils their immediate gratification and enjoyment, doesn't it? But you do this because the long-term benefits and rewards vastly outweigh the immediate greedy, thoughtless and short-term gratification of their desires.

Correct? I think so.

So another definition might be 'gratification postponement.' Not eating the *whole* bowl of jelly right now. Eating some and saving the rest for the next few days. Not because it's 'naughty' to eat all the jelly. Not because it's 'wicked or sinful' to eat all the jelly and God will slap your wrists. It's because if you eat all the jelly now, your enjoyment will be, say, ten units (8 for the one bowl, plus 16 for the rest of the jelly, minus 6 for the sick feeling, minus 8 for the realisation that you're a spineless worm with no will-power!).

If you have one bowl now, one tomorrow, and one the next day, you get 8+8+8 = 24 units of pleasure, plus 6 units for feeling smug about your strength of will. That's 30 units of pleasure compared with 10 units.

I'm not fooling around with this jelly analogy. This is exactly the way it works.

Disciplined people save money. They don't spend every single penny they have in their pockets on goodies to consume right now, as fast as possible. They don't then rush out and borrow more money to buy more goodies to consume because they can't wait until next pay day. Such people are eating all the sweets in one sitting, then borrowing sweets from their friends so they can eat those too! What would you say to a child who did that?

Why, what a spoilt and greedy child that would be, don't you think?

One of the keys to a successful life (*however* you define it) is the ability known as 'gratification postponement.'

The name speaks for itself and many people learn this ability and its advantages quite early on in life. At its most fundamental, it is the ability not to eat all the sweets today, in order that you will have some left over for tomorrow. As you grow up, it manifests itself in several ways. For example:

1. As a child: Your ability to delay playtime until you have completed all of your homework.

2. As a teenager: The ability to postpone the advantages of cash in your pocket *right now* from some mundane job. Instead you do further study so that you might enjoy a higher salary later on. Every hour of study you do gears up through your life to an effective rate of £1,000 for each study hour - but paid *later,* not right now.

3. As an adult: The ability not to spend every penny of the money you earn on goodies, but instead to save a percentage so that it might grow and you can enjoy more goodies later on.

Before I proceed, let me tell you there is nothing ascetic in what I am describing. The point is not to deny yourself forever and always postpone pleasure, possibly even until you die. That is ridiculous. No, the point is to enjoy today with all of its richness and pleasure, but to master the trick of gratification postponement for a percentage of life's pleasures. And this has only one, entirely selfish aim - to enjoy more of life's pleasures tomorrow. I want to be very clear on that point.

Many religions preach that you should deny yourself pleasure because it distracts you from your true task which is to sacrifice yourself for others and for God. Your reward, they say, will come when you die. Sorry, but that's just too long to wait, and too late to collect it.

For example, I consider the savings habit to be an absolute give-away sign of success or potential success. To save takes discipline - the discipline not to spend every penny you earn, but instead to put a little by. Most people do not save. They cannot manage the trick of postponing the gratification which the immediate use of their money would bring, consequently, they are always broke and struggling for cash.

Disciplined people don't save money out of altruism or because they are being good little boys or girls. They do it from a position of 'enlightened self-interest' or selfishness, by another name. It's important that you realise this. You're doing it for you, nobody else. They know that if they take some pleasure now (spend some money), then postpone the rest of the pleasure for a later day, they will get far more pleasure in total than if they spent all the money in one go. Everyone knows this. It's something we all learn at about age eight. It's part of the curriculum taught at the 'University of the Obvious!' Disciplined people apply this knowledge - it takes will-power not to spend the lot right now - undisciplined people just can't keep their hands out of the sweetie-jar, and that's the plain truth.

Modest saving - just 10% of your wealth - means you can retire with a quarter of a million in the bank. Nice.

Not saving means you retire penniless and with about five hundred pound's worth of useless junk. What a difference!

All successful people score highly on their ability to delay gratification, and research backs this up. Daniel Goleman in his remarkable book

Emotional Intelligence (ISBN 0-553-37506 - 7) quotes the following amazing study, which I'm sure you will find illuminating:

The 'Two Marshmallow' Test

Just imagine you are four years old and someone makes the following proposal: if you can wait until after he runs an errand, you can have two marshmallows for a treat. If you can't wait until then, you can have only one - but you can have it right now. It is a challenge sure to try the soul of any four year old, a microcosm of the eternal battle between impulse and restraint, id and ego, desire and self-control, gratification and delay. Which of these choices a child makes is a telling test; it offers a quick reading not just of character, but of the trajectory that a child will probably take through life.

There is perhaps no psychological skill more fundamental than resisting impulse. It is the root of all emotional self-control, since all emotions by their very nature, lead to one or another impulse to act.

A remarkable study in which the marshmallow challenge was posed to four-year-olds shows just how fundamental is the ability to restrain the emotions and so delay impulse. Begun by psychologist Walter Mischel during the 1960s at a pre-school on the Stanford University campus and involving mainly children of the Stanford faculty, graduates and other employees, the study tracked down the four-year-olds as they were graduating from high school.

Some four-year-olds were able to wait what must surely have seemed an endless fifteen to twenty minutes for the experimenter to return. To sustain themselves in their struggle, they covered their eyes so they wouldn't have to stare at temptation, or rested their heads in their arms, talked to themselves, sang, played games with their hands and feet, even tried to go to sleep. These plucky pre-schoolers got the two marshmallow reward. But others, more impulsive, grabbed the one marshmallow, almost always within seconds of the experimenter's leaving the room on his 'errand.'

The diagnostic power of how this moment of impulse was handled became clear some twelve to fourteen years later, when these same children were tracked down as adolescents. The emotional and social difference between the grab-the-marshmallow pre-schoolers and their gratification-delaying peers was dramatic.

Those who had resisted the temptation at four were now, as adolescents, more socially competent, personally effective, self assertive and better able to cope with the frustrations of life.

They were less likely to go to pieces, freeze or regress under stress, or become rattled or disorganised when pressured; they embraced challenges and pursued them instead of giving up, even in the face of difficulties; they were self-reliant and confident, trustworthy and dependable; they took initiative and plunged into projects. And, more than a decade later, they were still able to delay gratification in pursuit of their goals.

Those who grabbed for the marshmallow, however, tended to have fewer of these qualities, and shared instead a relatively more troubled psychological portrait. In adolescence, they were more likely to be seen as shying away from social contacts; to be stubborn and indecisive; to be easily upset by frustrations; to think of themselves as bad or unworthy; to regress or become immobilised by stress; to be resentful and mistrustful about not 'getting enough'; to be prone to jealousy and envy; to overreact to irritation with a sharp temper, so provoking arguments and fights. And after all those years, they were still unable to put off gratification.

What shows up in a small way early in life, blossoms into a wide range of social and emotional competence as life goes on. The capacity to impose a delay on impulse is at the root of a plethora of efforts, from staying on a diet to pursuing a medical degree. Some children, even at four, have mastered the basics: they were able to read a social situation as one where delay was beneficial, to pry their attention from focusing on the temptation at hand, and to distract themselves while maintaining the necessary perseverance toward their goal - the two marshmallows.

Even more surprising, when the tested children were evaluated again as they were finishing High School, those who had waited patiently at four were far superior as students to those who had acted on whim.

According to their parent's evaluations, they were more academically competent, better able to put their ideas into words, to use and respond to reason, to concentrate, to make plans and follow through on them and more eager to learn. Most astonishingly, they had dramatically higher scores on their SAT tests. Those who at four had grabbed for the marshmallow most eagerly had an average verbal score of 524 and quantitative (or 'math') score of 528. Those who had waited longest had average scores of 610 and 652 respectively - <u>a 210 point difference in total score</u>.

At age four, how children do on this test of delay of gratifications is twice as powerful a predictor of what their SAT scores will be as is IQ at age four. IQ becomes a stronger predictor of SAT scores only after children learn to read. This suggests that the ability to delay gratification contributes powerfully to intellectual potential, quite apart from IQ itself.

Poor impulse control in children is also a powerful predictor of later delinquency; again more so than IQ. What Walter Mischel, who did the study, describes as 'goal-directed self imposed delay of gratification' is perhaps the essence of emotional self-regulation: the ability to deny impulse in the service of a goal, whether it be building a business, solving an algebraic equation, or pursuing the Stanley Cup. His findings underscore the role of emotional intelligence as a meta-ability, determining how well or poorly people are able to use their other mental capacities.

Thanks to Daniel Goleman for that amazing insight.

Before I continue, I want to sound a word or two of warning. The problem with studies like the one Daniel Goleman describes is that you have to be careful about exactly what is causing the measured results.

Here are just four thoughts I had whilst reading Daniel's account - doubtless there are a dozen other possibilities:

1. The 'didn't grab' children could have come from severe and restrictive families who placed a disproportionate emphasis on manners and politeness thus inhibiting those children from greedily grabbing for a sweet without saying 'please' and 'thank you.' Perhaps such families could also be strong disciplinarians, forcing children to do their homework to a high standard and on time, etc. In other words, it is the family background causing the increase in ability and better SAT scores, not some inherent ability to resist gratification.

2. By a similar argument, the 'grab-a-marshmallow' children could have come from relatively deprived homes where treats were rare or non existent. That marshmallow was just so much more tempting to these children than to the other children who perhaps have plates of the sweets lying around all day, just for the taking.

3. Perhaps the 'grabbing' children came from larger families and had many siblings. Perhaps they have learned, even at age four, that if you don't grab it *now* (e.g. a biscuit) the plate will be empty in about three seconds! These poorer and more deprived children could do worse in life purely as a function of those factors (less parental time spent with them, etc.).

4. The 'didn't-grab' children might have been indifferent to marshmallows, or actively disliked them. The 'grab' children might have had a passion for marshmallows.

Having said this, the ability to resist impulse is still a powerful predictor of achievement and well-being, no matter how the ability arose (i.e. whether it was learned, imposed or somehow inherited).

I have to add my own experience in here.

After many years of teaching success principles to thousands of people, the one factor I would isolate in particular as being at the root of poverty and frustration is 'indiscipline.'

Put another way, successful people are disciplined - and one characteristic of a disciplined mind is the ability to postpone pleasure temporarily. Discipline, many times, means doing what you don't particularly want to do right now, in order that you can gear-up your efforts and have a far better future. That future sure comes around fast, and those 'lucky' disciplined people who were able to keep their hands off the sweeties, are soon able to enjoy their two marshmallow reward. Meanwhile the 'grab-a-marshmallow' gang look on in envy at the 'lucky' people with two marshmallows and are often bitter about the unfair state of the world in which some people seem to have two 'marshmallows' and some have only one.

As an aside, they almost certainly then vote for politicians who promise to steal marshmallows *by force* from people with 'too many' and distribute them free to the 'needy.'

It's Not Just Money

Discipline produces success even if your definition of success has nothing to do with money.

If your idea of success is to be a great pianist or painter or gardener, then to get there you must postpone immediate trivial pleasure such as watching TV or going out to the pub. Instead you must practice the piano, study painting, or weed the garden ready for the spring. I would submit that even if your definition of success was to be at peace with the world and to be in a blissful connected state with the universe you must first practice the long hours of discipline required for meditation, *and* practice the minute-by-minute discipline of pushing out the constant chatter of thoughts from your mind. A Zen monk, for example, could be said to be almost perfectly (and excessively) disciplined.

I think unsuccessful people are often that way because they have these two characteristics:

1. They rarely think of the future or plan for it. They live only for today.

Self-development guru Jim Rohn's secret of happiness is 'enjoying today whilst planning for a better tomorrow,' and this is a subject I explore further in the last chapter.

Living for the moment is only half of the story. You can only enjoy today because of the plans you made or work you did 'yesterday.' Similarly you can only enjoy tomorrow because of the plans you make or work you do today. This includes simple pleasures like a day walking in the countryside listening to the birds sing. You can only do that because 'yesterday' (last year, etc.) you worked hard enough and saved some money so that you could take time off. It is obvious that you can only eat today because of the work you did yesterday, unless you have set up your life to sponge from others.

2. They spend every single penny they earn (and usually more) on pleasures *right now, today*, and do not put anything away for the future.

This is similar to being given a week's worth of sweets and eating them all in one sitting!

Disciplined people use their time and talents to create present and future wealth for themselves. This means getting out of the armchair and doing something. This is hard. This takes effort and it takes will-power. Undisciplined people watch soap operas three times a week, go down the pub all the time (a net outflow of money), go out for meals, buy all the latest toys or generally fritter away their time and talents for thirty of forty years. And then.... huge surprise...they're broke when they retire!

Look, this hardly needs saying. There's nothing wrong with watching television sometimes, going down the pub now and then and having the odd meal out. These are pleasures. This is jelly now. Then, you turn the TV off and get to work on projects which will make you wealthy. You stay in several nights and work through until midnight on the same thing. This is investing time in your future, and is an identical concept to investing (saving) money for your future.

A disciplined person does not spend all his/her time now, in trivial pleasures, they save some for the future. Time is funny stuff. You can't put it in a box and save it for a future day, say the end of your life, and then haul it out and get extra days of life. The rule with time is that you have to invest it straight away. It multiplies and produces money in the future. You use this money to buy time from other people. For example, the money releases you from the need to work, and so that gives you a whole lot of time - much more than your original investment of time. Or, you use the money to pay someone to do your garden or your DIY, and that frees up a whole lot of time for more pleasurable things.

So the analogy is exact. Undisciplined people squander all their free time now on pleasures (eat all the jelly) and get, say, 100 units of pleasure. Disciplined people use a little of their time for pleasures (eat a little jelly now), then invest their time for the future. This multiplies many fold, and frees up vast amounts of time in the future. The net result is that they get (say) 1,000 units of pleasure in total over the years. This is their reward for being disciplined. I hope this makes sense.

The Rot Starts Early

Any failed or mediocre life is permeated through from top to bottom with lack of discipline, and it starts early. Here is a life report from one such man:

Failed at school because of lack of discipline (*always* mucked around instead of working; *always* out with the mates instead of doing some homework). Due to poor school results, got mediocre job. Never had a decent pay rise because lack of discipline meant he was often late for work and never did the job properly; always clock-watching and never went the extra mile. Never saved a penny - always spent the lot (and more) as soon as it came in. Never invested time for a better future, 'spent' the lot on trivial pleasures. Always in debt, never solvent - it takes discipline to control your finances. Retired - broke, bitter, disillusioned...and *surprised* at his poverty!

This needn't happen to you. Everyone has a sense of discipline. Heck, without it, you'd never get out of bed in the morning. Discipline is exactly that voice which says to you after the alarm has gone off: "Right, come on, up you get!" Without that, you'd just lie in bed all day. The trick is to start cultivating that sense of discipline - that small voice which nags away at you. You need to make it habitual. Don't suppress it. Listen to it and follow it. This is the difference between success and failure. The 'secret magic formula' of getting rich can be encapsulated in the quality of self-discipline. It's little more than that.

As an example, if you were disciplined enough to go out cleaning windows on a Saturday (or a few evenings a week) instead of frittering away your time, then after ten years of doing this and investing the money you would have £100,000 in the bank! I mention this not to encourage you to start a window cleaning round, but to prove that you don't need to start a stockbroking business, or open a chain of restaurants to make money. A simple piece of self-discipline in a lowly profession makes you a £100K in ten years, £300K in twenty years! Imagine what would happen if you *really* applied your talents! The only thing which stops people doing this is lack of self-discipline, or laziness by another name.

Be Disciplined in Small Things

Your future life is governed by a series of choices which you make. Little choices. Hourly, daily, weekly choices. Most people *always* choose the 'jelly now' option. This route leads to failure, I promise you that. Every little choice they make is an 'instant gratification' choice - to watch another hour of TV, to sleep late again, to go down the pub again, to have some entertainment, to lie in at the weekend, to buy some more goodies, to book a holiday they can't afford, and so on.

Life, you know, is incredibly short. Those of you over forty will know this already; those between 30 and 40 will be glimpsing the truth of this, and those under 30 probably still think they are immortal. I certainly did!

But, you know, the rewards of life come to the doers, not the talkers. This is so true. You receive riches from life in direct proportion to the amount of effort you put in. True again.

There is no 'miracle' short cut to wealth - basically, it's about getting off one's backside and actually *fighting, daring and winning* against the system.

That's really it.

It's a fight now, just as it was a hundred years ago, or a thousand years ago, for that matter. The rules have changed, but the game remains the same.

You need a better life and more money? Here's an important key to wealth:

Life doesn't respond to needs, wishes or desires. It laughs straight back in your face. Only your disciplined effort right now will plant the seeds of future crop which will meet your needs.

To complain that your needs should be filled right now is effectively to say: *"I have needs. Someone else should work and slave so that my needs might be provided for."*

What would the soil say to your statement *"I need some corn"*? Why, the answer would be *"Bring me your seed and your sweat!"* The soil would not care a finger snap for your needs. Who cares about your needs? Nobody. Furthermore the seed alone is not enough, is it? You must also plant, tend, water and hoe it.

These activities can be summed-up by the phrase 'disciplined effort.' Effort means the sweat of your brow; discipline means meticulously and regularly applied. A little each day. Gradually. This is how the rewards build up over the years. Not in a rush. You don't hoe, weed and water all in one day and expect a bumper crop the next. No, it doesn't work like this. You hoe a little one day, weed the next, water when it's dry, then go right back to hoeing.

Sounds like hard work? Welcome to the real world!

Nothing Comes From Nothing

Plant nothing, and get...nothing.

Spend all your money and save nothing, later in life you have...nothing.

Fritter your time away in trivia instead of learning - then, when you really need a skill or knowledge for that important job, you reach into your bag and pull out...nothing.

Work to the clock and never go the extra mile - when 'pay rise day' comes around then expect...nothing.

What's the magic solution for growing an instant crop? The crop you need *now* because you are hungry and couldn't be bothered to plant the seed and do the work? Farmer Giles would scratch his head and say: *"Buggered if I can think o' one, m'dear."*

And he's right. There is no magic solution. There is a long term solution and that is to learn the habit of discipline and make it your master. It can be done. Start with the small things and build up gradually until you become a powerful, self-disciplined person.

Successful people are disciplined. They choose some pleasure now, but will then choose hard work and effort over further immediate pleasure - this sows the seeds in order that they can reap a richer future harvest. They become successful and wealthy people.

Are you willing to give this route a try – *now*?

Chapter Six
You Must be Prepared to Pay the Price

"Self-made Millionaires Achieved This Status Because They Were Willing to Pay the Price."

There is a price to pay for getting rich, just as there is a price to pay for everything you attain in your life. Many chatter about being willing to pay the price, but few will actually do so. If you are serious about becoming a wealthy man or woman, you need to be prepared to pay the considerable price tag associated with that blissful state. It doesn't come free.

So let's talk honestly, frankly and openly about exactly what is involved if you are to make your fortune. You will not read what I am about to tell you in any 'feel good' book.

To make a lot of money, you're going to have to give up many things. A proper family life, a decent social life, friends and many other things besides. Often you won't even know what the price is when you start out. Nevertheless, you must resolve to pay it. This is the factor which stops most people from getting rich. They want it for nothing and are not willing to sacrifice anything at all to get it. This is a fantasy.

I think my strength is in smashing illusions, fantasies, and myths. Most people sign up for a great many of these fantasies which they believe to be 'the truth' and this has a huge impact on their wealth-creating efforts. Often it even threatens survival.

Most people barely survive financially. Worse still, lacking an iron-grip control on even the basics of their lives, they mumble the incantations of success, expecting magical results. That is, results which do not exact a price or penalty.

Let us be brutally honest here, this is the state of people in the United Kingdom today:

1. 2% are wealthy.

2. 5% are comfortable. They live in a decent house with a small or zero mortgage, they drive a new car, they take one or two holidays each year.

They have enough money for most of the things they need, but they are not wealthy. I would describe them as being in the high end of their comfort zone.

3. 53% are scraping along day-to-day, month to month. They are just about paying their way, but there is never any money left over for luxuries. Also, they live in constant fear of the large unexpected bill, tax demand, or medical expense. They are hanging on to the tricky business of life by the fingernails - barely surviving; lurching from crisis to crisis.

4. 40% are days away from drowning and are coming up for air for the third time. Their past mistakes and failures have created a crippling burden of debt which they have not the slightest hope of paying back through working at a normal job. The crushing weight of their errors and the cumulative effect of years of laziness, inaction and lack of discipline have created a terminal situation. Each month they sign up again for inaction and myopia. Each month their load becomes a little heavier. Without urgent and immediate action, the outcome is inevitable - *total financial collapse.*

As an aside, I would like you to reread the above paragraph and notice how I place the blame for this situation squarely on the shoulders of the person experiencing it. This is where it belongs of course but it is unfashionable to say so.

In a society which seeks to crush individualism and make each one of us a worker in the state collective, how can an *individual* possibly be to blame for his own misfortune? He cannot. This would give the individual some personal power, and that cannot be right! No. It must be society, greedy capitalists, manipulative industry, bad luck, his upbringing, peer pressure, his race, lack of education, his age, lack of opportunity, or any one of a hundred other factors all of which are out of his control. In short, he is not to blame, according to modern thinking.

If you doubt this, read the following and see if it has a familiar ring:

"Yes, I admit it. I'm flat broke and I owe tens of thousands of pounds to other people which, to be honest, I don't have a prayer of paying back. But it's not my fault. I was made redundant from my job and thrown on the scrap heap at 40. Those greedy bosses call it downsizing - but I don't notice any downsizing in their fat wallets. Twenty years I've worked there, and that's all the thanks I get. I'm a heavy- motor electrical engineer, and there just aren't that many jobs around for someone of my abilities. I've applied for a few but they always want younger men. I guess losing my job made me kinda depressed and my wife couldn't take it. She wants a divorce and the bitch is taking me for every penny. I don't have any savings, and the money I get from the state is a joke. Sure I'm broke, but as you can see it's not my fault."

Blame-Shifting

Let me translate this litany of blame shifting.

"I am such a weak and feeble human being, that I have been unable to master one of the simplest and most basic skills of life; that is to spend less than I earn. My greed exceeds my means to pay for it, and so to fuel my desires, I must borrow from the surplus created by others. I have spent every penny of my own money, and squandered the surplus created by others which they entrusted to me on the promise that I would pay them back. I have broken that trust and they are unlikely to get their money. I am not a trustworthy human being, but it's not my fault.

"I know that the world is a dangerous and uncertain place, but for twenty years I decided to ignore that fact. Consequently I have zero savings, but it isn't my fault. I needed all the stuff I bought, and a lot more besides. I did some training once, twenty years ago, and I fully expected that to last forty years.

"The world owes me a living, and society should provide jobs for people with my abilities, regardless of whether they are needed or not. Bosses should provide jobs for workers regardless of profits. People need jobs, and it is the duty of bosses to provide them. I have no intention of retraining. I have made a half-hearted attempt to get another job, but because I'm so weak, I get quickly discouraged and so I have given up. Now I get free money from the state. This is nothing like enough for me to live on, and I think the state should give me a lot more free money."

I know you do not hold the same attitudes as this man - you would not be reading this book if you did!

So given the terrible poverty, both financial and spiritual of the majority of people, what can you do to raise yourself up into the top 2% (by Western standards)? How can you achieve this success?

This fifth secret is all about realising that you cannot have it all, and that you must pay a big price (give up something) in order to attain wealth. You need to be crystal clear in your own mind that you are willing to pay the price, otherwise abandon all hopes right now of becoming rich.

It is vital that you apply full focus to this very important area if you are not to drift through life aimlessly.

You Cannot Have it All

So, it's time for some home truths. The first thing you have to know is that *you can't have it all.*

Despite what those slick-suited seminar-gurus tell you, every decision you take in life has a shadow partner - the life you cannot now lead because you took that decision.

A few simple examples will prove the point.

You take a career decision to become a surgeon; but doing this precludes you from being a lawyer.

As a woman you decide to marry and have a family. The consequence is that your career is on hold for a minimum of five years and more like fifteen or twenty.

You decide to go to the cinema; you cannot also spend the evening in a fine restaurant.

You decide to give up drinking; you cannot now go boozing with your pals.

You decide to start thinking for yourself; you lose most of your 'friends.'

Every decision you take has consequences.

Every decision, no matter how seemingly inconsequential, sets your life on a slightly different course. This is why, as Jim Rohn says, "Everything matters."

Even *inaction* has its consequences.

If you decide just to float down life's stream, and the current sweeps you randomly into the left tributary, you cannot also enjoy the right tributary. If you sleep all day, you cannot also play your favourite sport on that day.

This tiny handful of examples should prove to you immediately that you cannot have it all. It is so obvious that it is hardly worth saying, and yet there are at least two top seminar gurus on the circuit at the moment who are claiming that you can. In fact, I'm fairly certain that I have seen a book and a tape series entitled "You CAN have it all." Wrong! But far more importantly, every decision you take to improve your life, no matter how trivial, will have an associated cost - a price that you will have to pay in order to achieve that success.

The price usually involves the sacrifice of one aspect of your life, in order to achieve more in your main area of endeavour.

Here's a simple example. You're a single guy, and you decide to spend every evening for the next three months decorating and improving your house from top to bottom in order that you might sell it for the best price. This will allow you to realise your goal of moving up the housing market. You really want a detached house and have a burning desire to move out of the poverty-stricken terraced-house neighbourhood in which you live. Great goal! But the principle is that you can't have it all, so what is the price that you will pay for choosing this route?

Answer: It will kill your social life for the next three months. No drinking, no clubbing, no frittering away your time with the mates. Who knows, you might have met your future wife at one of those missed evenings at the club, but instead you were home, working.

The pathways of your life divide. You follow one which leads to a brighter, better tomorrow - according to your best judgement, of course. The other diverges sharply, blinks and shimmers uncertainly before fading out to join the countless millions of other 'might have beens.' You never meet that woman, you never marry and have children with her.

Another example: Charles sets himself the goal of becoming super successful; really mega-rich. This man wants £100 million, he wants it badly and he's going to get it. Now that's a lot of money and far more than I will see in my lifetime, and I've seen plenty!

Now ask yourself seriously, can this man have it all?

Can he work the demanding 12 hour days, 350 days each year which are required to achieve this level of success and be a perfect father who never misses his son's football matches or his daughter's clarinet concert? Can he be a perfect husband who is always home from the office by 5:30 to peck his wife on the cheek; who's never late for a dinner party with friends? Can he shoot for super success and also be a competent odd-job man who spends weekends and evenings tinkering with the plumbing, or installing new work-surfaces, pipe clenched firmly between teeth?

Let's go further. Can he try for mega-wealth, and also be a 'good old mate' to a bunch of lads down at the local? Can he play for the darts' team Tuesdays and Thursdays? Can he say "yes" to a ten day skiing holiday with his friends? Is he likely to be an active member of his local choir or amateur dramatics group? The answer is no. Shooting for this level of wealth requires laser-beam focus. There will be late night and breakfast meetings; urgent problems to sort out requiring him to jump on a plane at a moment's notice; international midnight telephone calls - you name it.

Let us probe deeper. Will others consider him to be a reliable friend? In other words, are people likely to say of him *"Good old Charlie, he's a real pal. You've only got to pick up the phone any hour of the day or night and he's there for you."*?

I don't think so, do you?

Charles is on a fast track to super-success; this track is not open to any old mooch or bum, it requires extraordinary discipline and effort. It requires 100% commitment; and total dedication to the task in hand. This level of success commands a high price, not surprisingly, otherwise every half-witted, unfocused fool in the country would be doing it.

Whilst we are on the subject, let us ask: "Will Charles have many, or indeed *any*, friends?"

Friendship has a high time-overhead, in case you haven't noticed. You have to call each friend at least once a week and meet them at least once a fortnight, otherwise they fairly rapidly drop out of your circle of mates. With only a dozen chums, you will find that most evenings and weekends, indeed almost every spare moment you have, will be consumed in meeting friends for a drink, chatting on the telephone to catch up with all the gossip, coffee mornings, driving endlessly to and fro from their tiresome houses, dandling their squawking brats on your knee and going "coochy-coo," letter writing, e-mails and returning mutual favours.

Your life is thus reduced to working, sleeping, and *entertainment* (socialising). It would not be overstating the case to say that this describes most people's lives. There is nothing wrong with that, *if* the major life-goal you have set yourself is 'to be a good friend to as many people as humanly possible.' But can you do this *and* be a super success? Can Charles shoot for his hundred million, and be the person I just described? Can Charles have it all?

The answer is tritely obvious. No he cannot. If he is to achieve his dream, he must pay the price - and the price is a big one.

All Dreams Have Their Price

This doesn't just apply to Charles and his very high goal of making a hundred million. It is important for you to realise that every goal you set in life has an associated price which you will have to pay. Big dreams come with a large, fancy, gold-embossed price tag. Smaller goals have a cheap supermarket stick-on label, but there is still a price attached to every dream.

You cannot have it all.

I hope you have taken this on board, and now believe it totally. You cannot move beyond this point in the realisation of your dreams if even a small part of you still subscribes to the fantasy of being able to have it all. *You cannot.* Neither can you have something for nothing. You get no results in life unless you pay the price. No free lunches. No 'emanations from the bountiful universe.' Sorry - it doesn't work like that, much as we would all want it to. The universe is only bountiful as long as we put forth the required effort to make it fruitful. We only get a bumper crop from 'bountiful nature' by doing the backbreaking work of preparing the ground, planting the seed, weeding, hoeing and watering. All of this must be done before you can enjoy the harvest.

I am reminded of the story of the vicar walking through his village. He comes across a man working in a beautiful cottage garden. He stops to admire the lovely flowers and says: "I see that you and God have done a splendid job on your garden." To which the man replies: "Yes, you should have seen it when God had it all to himself!"

The Entrepreneur

To make serious money you almost certainly have to run your own business - and if you have never done this before, you are in for a shock!

Running a business is like standing on a shore with wave after wave of problems hitting you. It never stops. It never goes away. Some waves are tiddlers, some are like tidal waves, most are normal sized waves.

The variety and challenge in business comes in what particular set of problems you will face today. Yesterday it was a massive bad debt, today your supplier has gone bankrupt, tomorrow it will be some government jobsworth trying to shut you down. Next week it will be a VAT inspection, then employee sickness, followed by a fire inspection to ensure you have 3.6 extinguishers to every 19.3 employees. The week after that it's a problem at your printer followed in quick succession by your telephone system failing, the alarm system going off at 2 a.m. and an irate customer threatening to sue you for something he purchased from an entirely different company with a similar sounding name...

It just goes on and on. This is part of the price you pay, daily, weekly, yearly. It has been said with some truth that everyone makes money by solving other people's problems. I have not even mentioned the positive army of faceless bureaucrats with a strong anti-business agenda. The ASA, PIA, DMSB, MOPS, DTI, Trading Standards, DPA, SFA, MPS, FSA, Inland Revenue etc. etc. You have to be able to bat away all of these problems and come back for more without it destroying you. Making big money *is* all about handling hundreds of problems. Some easy, some total sons of bitches.

The truth is that many people can't handle this. I don't mean they are incapable - many problems are no-brainers. I mean that they are not willing to handle them - to pay the price for success. Most people's emotional bank account runs out long before their financial bank account. In other words, they can't handle the endless wave of problems and so they just roll over.

Another price you must pay is to be alienated from most people in the society you currently inhabit. Until now, you have probably been immersed in the warm, weak soup of British society. This will change. Are you willing to pay this price too?

The Painful Truth

Let me tell you some facts about the UK and its people, in general. As a race we have many wonderful characteristics. We are tolerant, kind, easygoing, industrious and have a profound sense of right and wrong, to name just a few. But there is a character trait of which I am not proud to be a part. Whilst most people play the lottery, have premium bonds, do the football pools and pray to get rich 'by accident or luck,' (i.e. for *zero effort*) they simultaneously loathe and despise anyone who has made something of their lives and will do anything to slap down such a person and destroy them. Read the tabloids if you doubt this. Anyone with more than £10,000 is called a 'Fat Cat' and anyone with a four bedroomed house apparently lives in a 'mansion.' E.g. 'Fat Cat Robert Smith was unavailable for comment when we visited his mansion in Surrey.'

If you ever make more than a modest amount of money or achieve fame, you face the distinct possibility of being attacked, ridiculed, smeared, and hounded by the press and media. Their sworn mission will be to drag you down - to find some dirt in your background, some chink in your armour which they can then use to destroy you. It's not personal, it's just because their readers want you destroyed.

Why?

Their readers detest successful people because they act like glittering beacons, lighting the steep, rocky pathway which leads from a life in the sheep pen, to a life of heroic excellence. A successful person, by merely existing, causes the average person to think: *"Oh no! This is terrible! If this ordinary guy can make a success of his life, that means..... that means..... perhaps I could improve my life too. Well I guess I now have two choices. I can apply the energy, discipline and focus required to follow him along the path to excellence. Or... I can scour the gutter press for evidence that this man is corrupt, that he is lower than me and really belongs in the sewer. Hmmm... now which is the easiest path...?"*

Please also remember you live in a socialist country, regardless of which party is currently in power. A socialist believes in seizing your hard-earned wealth under threat of imprisonment, and distributing it free to the needy masses. That description applies equally well to both parties. They merely tolerate active individuals like yourself, because they know that you produce the wealth to keep the whole caravan rolling along.

What else forms part of the price you must pay if you want tens of millions?

- You will have very few, *if any*, close friends. You just will not have the time to nurture and sustain lots of buddy-pal relationships.
- You will not be able to enjoy a normal family life. You might have children, but you will be a strange, remote, absent figure. Your family will not be able to rely upon you to attend weddings, funerals, birthday parties, concerts, plays and school open-days. Sometimes you'll be there - most times you won't.
- Most people you meet will be consumed by cancerous jealousy and hatred no matter how much they smile and praise you to your face. They will also not know or understand the price you paid to achieve success. They will think, and sometimes even say to your face, that you were 'lucky.' To them, wealth is just a lottery - an accident which happens 'to' some people and not to others, for various mysterious, unfathomable reasons. In their eyes, you just got lucky and now you are flashing it around.

- You will be under regular government surveillance, including the monitoring of your telephone. Why? Because money equals power, and a hundred million (for example) is a lot of power - almost enough to destabilise the country. You will be viewed as a threat to national security and a close eye kept on you. Governments do not like citizens to have power. In their mind, there is only one place for power to reside and that is with them, the government. Believe it! You will have a detailed file kept on you, together with information suitable for blackmailing you if you ever step out of line.
- You will work 12 hour days, 350 days of the year. You will eat, live, sleep and breathe your project. Every second spent away from the office or factory will seem like agonising torture. Read *'Atlas Shrugged'* by Ayn Rand and study the character of Hank Reardon if you want a superb description of how you must be. The company of others, even friends and family, will seem dull and you will be filled with an overwhelming craving to tear yourself away and return to your empire.
- You will be sued, attacked, spat upon, and will receive regular death threats, many of which are credible. You will require several full-time office staff to reply to the sacks full of whining, begging letters you will receive, to field the hundreds of weekly calls from charities and to stave off the hordes of religious fanatics entreating you to give up your 'evil' wealth and discover God.

To sum up, the world will simultaneously be trying to destroy you and mooch from you. If you do not believe this to be true, it is simply because you have never amassed enough money to see this start to happen.

That is just a tiny example of the price you will have to pay in order to get many millions.

Is this too high a price? Then don't write the goal down. You learned something. You *don't* want millions because you're not prepared to pay the price. There's no shame in this whatsoever. Set a far more modest, more achievable goal together with its associated lower price tag - one you can afford to pay.

As I mentioned in the chapter on goal-setting, please do not commit the gross error of writing down a big money goal (or any goal) in the hope that you will attain it by mystical methods; that somehow God, or the bountiful universe will cause this money to 'flow' to you. It won't, so please stop dreaming! This is one of the most common errors I see in people. It is obvious why. Signing up for this belief has two great advantages:

1. You don't have to do anything - the universe will do it all for you.

2. You can excuse your inaction because you are just waiting for 'your turn' - that moment when the universe (lady luck, etc.) deigns to smile in your direction and pour riches upon you.

Perhaps you think that £1-5 million will be easier?

Yes it will, but still you still have a huge price to pay and you must decide now if you are willing to pay it.

You will merely suffer a milder form of all of the consequences I mentioned above.

You will lose every single one of your current friends - trust me on this one. You will work 10 hour days, 330 days of the year. You will be a driven man or woman. Most, if not all of your other hobbies and interests will be sacrificed to this goal.

You enjoy sailing, skiing, flying, drama, bridge? Forget it! You won't have time. You always wanted to write a play, learn jazz piano, study water-colour painting, be an attentive parent or partner? These will have to wait. All of your energy, talent, and time will be devoted to achieving your goal of great wealth.

Many are tempted to think they would accept any hardship, any conditions, any price just so long as they got their hands on that lovely money, but I urge you to think this through very carefully. If you don't want to pay the price then don't write the goal.

Save yourself some heartache. You've learned something important. You don't want £1-5 million, leastways, you're not prepared to pay the price for it and that leaves you fresh out of trump cards. You only hold the four jokers - 'prayer,' 'luck,' 'bountiful flow of the universe' and 'hope.' On the basis of my sneaky peek at that load of rubbish, *I'll definitely raise you a hundred....*

So before you write a figure down on your 'money goal' card we mentioned in chapter 4, spend a few moments considering if you are willing to pay the price. If not, then you are deciding right now on a life of poverty.

At least you decided. That's far better than drifting into it and then wondering what went wrong. Having taken a firm decision you can immediately unclutter your mind. Like clearing out a garage you can throw away a lot of shoulds, oughts and 'one days.' You know that becoming rich is no longer an option for you, and this brings a certain amount of peace. You can now concentrate your energy and talents on more modest and hence achievable goals in your life.

To summarise this important chapter. Everything you obtain in life has a price tag attached to it. This includes material objects and more intangible things such as wisdom and experience. There is always a price. Before rushing headlong in to a ten or twenty year struggle to make your fortune, a wise man or woman would sit back for a while and think very carefully about whether or not they are willing to pay the price associated with this. The sacrifice is great, the rewards are great. Take an intelligent decision - the one which is right for you.

Chapter Seven
You Must Take Firm, Decisive Action

"Serious People Actually DO Something; Non-Serious People Talk About Doing Something or Plan to do Something One Day"

If you want to be wealthy, you must take action.

Action really is the key. You can have the best ideas in the world or be the most talented person on the planet, yet still if you do not take action you will remain poor. A half-wit who actually does something will beat an inactive genius, hands down.

You need to take action, but most people cannot master this one - it is far too hard for them.

We live in a physical world which has a tendency to decay into a random warm soup of molecules. This is entropy at work. Only energy, such as that supplied by living creatures, can reverse this process and build structures. Food, clothing, shelter, 'toys' - all require *energy* to make them exist. All require human action.

Without energy, all is dust and decay.

Thinking is not enough. To complete the equation, you must also act. You must do something.

Here is the startling two-step secret of success:

1. Think.
2. Act.

Most people do neither - in a concerted, meaningful way, I mean.

Some act without thinking. No good. Some think and never act. No good. The winners, the rich, the successful all think first, which usually means coming up with a creative solution to a human need, and then they put that idea into a tangible program of action. This is what you must do if you wish to join them.

Do you find this daunting? That's okay, there's no shame in this, but please, do yourself and everyone else a favour and *stop talking and thinking about 'one day' becoming wealthy.* This is a delusion because you are not prepared to pay the price we discussed in the last chapter. The price is thought followed by action, so if you want to become wealthy, then start now today. You've written your goals, now ask yourself what actual steps you can do, right now, today, to move you closer towards your dream.

Would you like to know two ways of getting rich apart from luck or crime? Remember, I'm talking here about getting rich, and not making a living. Anyone can make a living. Getting rich is far harder.

To become a wealthy man or woman, you must come up with an original, creative idea for a product or service which you believe the public will want to buy from you. Then you must put in the hours to research and test this idea. If it looks no good, you must create another idea until you find a winner. The second way is to locate a hot, fresh idea which is working somewhere right now (say in another country) and then to recreate the idea in your own territory, obviously without plagiarising somebody else's work. E.g. if you hear that a new premium rate telephone line on Irritable Bowel Syndrome is taking 19,000 calls a day in the USA, this is an idea you could immediately pick up and run with in the UK. In other words, you wait for someone else to find a winner, then jump *quickly* onto the bandwagon.

When you have found a winner, then you must pursue your idea and dream with *passion*, and not some wimpish and feeble 'attempt.' This is called 'paying the price.' The price is action and sometimes a little money. If you are broke, then you must chose an idea which doesn't take a lot of money.

If you don't feel passionate about your idea, then it's not for you. How do you think you're going to succeed at something you feel lukewarm about? What will drag you out of bed on those cold winter mornings? What will give you the courage to face those waves of problems we discussed? What will keep you fighting on when all about you is turning to ashes and you are filled with hopeless despair? Your lukewarm desire to 'have a go'? I don't think so!

An idea without action is almost worthless. So I would not try to go down the route of thinking up 'inventions' which you can sell to Black and Decker, etc. Only very rarely do such ideas get taken up, and even then you would not make a fortune. Instead, your idea should be one that *you* can operate and reap the rewards from. The more original the better, otherwise you are just picking over the bones of somebody else's idea, and you will not become wealthy. Even when you jump onto a new bandwagon, you still need creative energy to transform that idea into something which will work in your area. There is little money to be made when you are tenth out of fifty in the marketplace, with nothing to distinguish your product or service from that of your competitors.

When I tell people this stark truth during consultations, they often complain: "I don't have any ideas." "What can I do? I'm not really sure." "I've tried for *ages* to think of something, but I just come up with a blank." "Help me! Have *you* got any original ideas you don't want and which you can pass on to me?"

I know it's hard to be in this position - remember I was there too. Yes, it seems difficult; impossible sometimes, but this is what will mark you out as a winner if you can pass this initiation test.

Please let me be absolutely clear on this and give you the stark truth if you are also tempted to complain about not having any ideas.

You're not creative? You've never had an original thought in your life? You've tried a couple of times to think of something new, but given up? Well I have some very bad news for you. You will never be wealthy unless you win the lottery or get lucky in some other way. You will always be poor, struggling along with the masses, scarcely able to pay your way and probably in debt until the day you die. At the very best you will eke-out survival in a paid job, or rake over the dead ashes of somebody else's dream, hoping to raise the Phoenix, but the bird will have long since flown away.

I am sorry if I sound a little harsh, but I believe quite strongly that you would rather have the truth from me, bitter though it is, than to be fed more lies and distortions.

Reminder: These comments only apply to *getting rich*. It's okay not to want to be rich - really, it is - in which case this doesn't apply.

Wealth belongs to creative people alone. There is only one way to get honestly wealthy. Persuade lots and lots of people to give you their money. You can either do this at the point of a gun (dishonest), or you can offer them something which makes them give it to you voluntarily - to trade with you.

Now if you cannot muster the energy to come up with your own idea, or you think that you are 'not creative,' then guess what? - you pick up somebody else's fifth-hand idea and try to run that. Guess what again? Only a few people hand you their money, the rest trade with the *hundreds* of others who are all trying to run the same idea and you don't get rich! You just about make a living. This is not what you want, I hope.

Now if you take action and create something original and new, suddenly you're the only supplier. Thousands or millions of people flock to willingly exchange their money for your product or service and you become wealthy. More importantly, you become guiltlessly wealthy - you earned it through your creative endeavours.

We Are All Creative

Finally, everyone is creative. "I'm not creative" is often an excuse. If we are honest, it often means: "I'm lazy and can't be bothered to put in the hard work which I know this creative effort will cost me." Right? Remember I'm saying all of this for a very good reason, and that reason is not to attack you. I either want you to wake up, finally, to the fact that you are not prepared to do what it takes to get rich, or I want to jolt you into action so that you make a start towards your dream. That is my only motive and I'm sorry if sometimes what I say seems a little hard on you.

So let me make myself very clear. If you are not interested in becoming wealthy, then that's okay. There's nothing wrong with that, and none of these comments apply to you. I'm being sincere now when I say there's absolutely nothing wrong with earning a living, raising a family and doing all that other good stuff - or even sitting on a Zen mat all day meditating. Whatever makes you happy and fulfilled is fine because it's your life and your happiness we are talking about.

But if you have ever wanted to be rich or if you aspire to great wealth one day, then please listen closely to the message in this chapter. In fact read it again and again.

Above all, please wake up and stop dreaming. Ignore 'get rich quick' schemes and the like. Forget other people's 'off the shelf' ideas. Take action. Start doing something now, today to move you an inch closer to your dream. Not tomorrow - that's too late. If you can't work until midnight *tonight* to make a start on turning your dream into a reality, then the year will engulf you. It will be business as usual. The same old dull routine. Last year replayed.

I really do want you to succeed because I know how sweet is the taste of success. You will love it. So go for it and start taking decisive action.

This Might do the Trick

If you need a little guiding shove, I'm going to use the well known tactic of fear to see if I can initiate some action.

Let me remind you of something scary - this could be you.

Over 65% of people remain poor throughout their entire lives; they retire penniless or in debt and they die broke and embarrassed. That is, after a *lifetime* of hard slog, usually in a job they detest, they manage to accumulate... nothing. They are able to leave...nothing. Their entire assets amount to...nothing. There are a few cheap sticks of furniture, some photographs, a heap of rubbish in the loft and that's it. The whole lot would fit into a large skip - but generally it's just tossed onto a bonfire by 'house clearance specialists.' A quick coat of emulsion, and the house is ready for the next person - all trace of the previous occupant having been eradicated. It wasn't hard. There was little to eradicate.

A few people attend the funeral - mostly people press-ganged by the immediate family into coming to swell the numbers. A few years later only a handful of people remember anything about the deceased. A funny story (from thirty years ago, usually) a brief recollection; a fleeting image triggered by a place or a melody.

Soon, there is nobody left who remembers; there is only a name on a cheap plaque in the 'garden of remembrance.' The person fades into obscurity to join the teeming billions of others who were born, lived, reproduced and died. They did not push mankind forward one iota. They left the planet just slightly worse than they found it due to the resources they consumed but otherwise, the entire effect of their lives was...zero.

Why am I telling you this depressing story? Because I don't want you to become one of these faceless billions. You are special. The horrifying truth is that each one of those 'faceless' billions was special too, they just did not realise it or do anything about it during their lifetime.

In the past perhaps there was some excuse. Opportunities were harder to come by. People were born into poverty and negativity. They were not exposed to motivational materials: society, religion and family conspired to keep them locked into servitude. They worked down at the mill and married the girl or boy next door. Resistance was useless. Escape was almost impossible.

But you don't have this excuse. You live in the most startling, incredible decade in the entire history of the human race - and that is not even close to an exaggeration, it is an obvious fact. There are more opportunities, more wealth-generation potential, more chances than at any previous time since the dawn of man. That too, is a plain fact. If you can't make it in this climate, in this country, in this decade then I can absolutely guarantee that you will stay in, or join the 65% - broke and embarrassed.

Believe me, you don't want to be retired and broke in the coming years - it will not be fun. You are not going to get a state pension worth having - not that it ever was worth having. If you do not start to take action, you will be left behind. Within twenty years, the number of retired people will far outstrip society's ability to care for them - financially or medically. If you are over forty, then THIS MEANS YOU! If you are under forty, prepare to be taxed even harder to support the insupportable.

So how do you get started? What is the way forward?

Here are some guiding lights to help you on the path:

Ten Tips To Making a Million

I prefer being rich to poor, and I've tried both. I used to think that being a millionaire was for other people - for me it seemed just a ridiculous dream. I'm telling you this to show you that I've been exactly where you are right now. I am merely further up the mountain path than you. I am not unchaseable, indeed I invite you to overtake me! Come on up, the air is cleaner and fresher here, I can promise you that. My ten tips for making a lot of money are as follows:

1. Do something. That's what this chapter is all about. Don't sit around any longer. Forget TV, forget the pub; start taking action to improve your life, even if it is just that first, small step. I judge people by what they do rather than what they say.

2. Be rationally selfish. Take 'good for me' decisions. You don't *owe* anything to anyone apart from your kids. They need love, consistency and honesty. They don't need Adidas trainers and Nintendo games machines. When you live your life trying to take 'good for others' decisions, you are playing God and trying to second-guess other people's lives. This is arrogant.

3. Stop believing in something for nothing. This one tip can save you thousands of pounds and a lot of lost time. There is no such thing as something for nothing. Ditch all of those 'business opportunities' which come your way. 99% of them are scams operated by small minded people of limited vision trying to cheat their way to a fortune. They are relying upon your laziness and gullibility. Don't support them, and above all, don't join them. The financial loss is minimal, but the loss of time and momentum is far more serious.

4. You should have one burning question which you must answer as soon as possible: *"What honest value can I create which others will voluntarily buy from me time and time again in order that I might become guiltlessly wealthy?"*

Only you can answer this question and you must work at it rather than expecting the answer for nothing. Nobody is going to hand you a wonderful, magic pre-packaged business on a plate. It's obvious why. If you had some superb practical 'make a million' business, would you operate it yourself and make a million, or sell a 30-page 'how to' manual for £24.95 to a few hundred punters via an advert in Exchange and Mart?

5. When you *create* values you become wealthy. When you *trade* equal values you merely survive. There is nothing wrong with survival. Most people do only this. But make sure you have consciously selected this option, and not chosen it by default out of laziness or fear.

Most businesses merely allow you to trade values - "You watch my sheep and I'll mend your roof" - and so you will not become wealthy by operating one of the 10,000 or so businesses you might think about getting involved in. For example, "I'll cook fish and chips if you repair my car." At best, you will do slightly better than average due to the division of labour and your superior bartering skills, but you will never make a million.

To become wealthy you must create new values which didn't exist before and then run with your idea until the copycats grab your idea and rake over the bones of your fortune. Then you have another, new idea which creates more unique values and you run with that... These ideas do not have to be earth-shattering; many are just small creative twists on an existing idea.

Most small businesses don't create new values, they merely trade existing values. This is the main reason the proprietors never get wealthy.

6. Remember that honest wealth is not gained at the expense of others. In other words, contrary to socialist doctrine, other people do not become poorer as you become richer (but this *is* how looters operate). By trading with you, they should become a little richer whilst you become a lot richer. Evaluate all business ideas by this standard: *"Does this business allow me to trade with others whilst enriching their lives, or am I trying to scam, con, cheat and lie my way to wealth? Am I using smoke and mirrors to pretend there is a benefit to my customers, when no such benefit really exists?"*

7. Anything can be justified by the clever human brain. Robbery can be justified: "It's not fair that some people have so much money, I'm just redistributing wealth. In a fairer society I wouldn't have to do this." Cheating can be justified: "I'm giving people the expensive education they need in gullibility. I am helping them to become less gullible." Even murder can be justified: "We're all going to be dead soon anyway, so what's the difference?" In view of this ability to justify and evil-doing, you need to keep your business clean and make sure it follows your own impeccable standards.

8. Make *yourself* wealthy - don't have as your motivation the desire to make others wealthy or to improve their lot. This will not work unless you are being conned, by religion for example. The feeling of being a good little boy or girl is not enough to sustain you through the difficult task ahead (making yourself rich). Operating in the way I have described (by creating values which others will want from you) will both make you wealthy and improve the living standards of those around you. Everyone is a winner. But if you have altruism as your doctrine - the idea that you are a sacrificial animal only fit for consumption by others - then you will live a powerless, unfulfilled life as a slave or an interfering, do-gooder busybody. When you have filled your own needs, then you become powerful enough to help others, if this gives you pleasure.

9. Don't listen to broke people. They know nothing about money. If they were merely neutral, it wouldn't matter, but they are not. Your friends, your family, society, the media and the government all want you broken back down to drone status, *no matter what they say or how much they protest to the contrary.* There is one person you can really trust on this wild adventure and that is *you*. You doubt this? See what happens when you start making a bit of money and buy a new house or car. This is a general rule about people - there are, of course, exceptional people out there, like you, who will support you. They are a rare breed so cherish them.

10. You must be prepared to pay the price, whatever it is, for becoming wealthy. There is always a price. You can't get rich for nothing. Most often the price is hard work, tenacity, guts, determination and effort. Little more is needed to succeed in our society because so few people have these characteristics. The rewards are unlimited wealth, guiltless affluence, freedom from stress, power and the feeling of leading a meaningful worthwhile life. The last of these is the most important, and no lottery win can buy you that feeling. It comes only from creating lasting worthwhile values which enrich the lives of your fellow human beings.

Right Here, Right Now

It is time, right now, to snap out of it and get your sleeves rolled up. The excuses are over. You have read the books, listened to the tapes, subscribed to the newsletters, but what have you *done*?

Are you a man or woman of action? Do you 'walk the talk' or are you just an armchair dreamer? People who only dream live broke and die broke. Yes, it all starts with a dream but for the dream to be meaningful, it must be made manifest in this physical world. To achieve this, you must act.

Do you collect motivational material for show, or do you actually use it? The users succeed in life, the readers stay the same as they always were.

Are you a procrastinator, always putting off until tomorrow those things which you know you should start today? These people have small goals and achieve little of import during their lifetime.

Are you waiting for your boat to come in? Are you pinning your hopes on winning the lottery or the pools? You'll still be waiting aged eighty, huddled in front of your one-bar electric fire in some grim council high-rise flat.

This book is your wake-up call. If I were with you now, I would snap my fingers in your face in a particularly irritating manner - enough to make you want to sock me a good one. If I thought it would do any good I'd shake you too! *Anything* - anything at all to get you to wake up to the following facts:

1. You're getting older. Time is running out.

2. You're BROKE, by any sensible definition of the word. Furthermore, unless you snap out of it and start taking some action, you'll be broke when you retire (not nice...not nice at all) and broke when you die. And this, in the golden decade of unlimited opportunity. You should be ashamed of yourself!

3. Unless you start to make serious changes, you are going to leave absolutely nothing of value behind when you go. I'm not talking money here. I'm talking *contribution*. Something to be remembered by. I don't care what. A book, a poem, a business, a piece of music, an idea...*something*.

Now don't get cute with me and start disputing point number two. You're broke. Take my word for it. I don't care if you've got a few thousand in a building society deposit account, or if you've got a trifling fifty grand equity in your house. I don't care if you're running a little business or even if you're moderately successful, you're still poor. Unless you have about £3 million, then you're poor. Any money under this amount is fiddling small change and you'd better start believing it if you want a life of power, wealth and passion.

Carefully note those three words. There are alternatives to a life of power, wealth and passion and here are two alternatives:

➤ The tree-hugger who believes that a life passed in quiet contemplation of the eternal is a life well spent.
➤ The minimalist life - one in which you rely on the absolute minimum money required for bare survival because anything else seems a bit of a strain. This lifestyle allows you to potter in some inconsequential manner. Such a life is squandered in bumbling amongst a pile of trivia.

Of course both of these options are valid lives, if you have actively chosen them for correct, positive reasons, but if either lifestyle describes you, then why you are reading this book is a mystery to me! It's probably part of your collection - you know, the motivational materials you buy in order to fool yourself that you're actually doing something, when you're not. I'm sorry - did that hit a little too close to home?

If I sound impassioned - believe it! It would be far easier for me to write a warm, wet and human book in which I give you a nice little pat on the back for your efforts to date.

Here is some more of that unpalatable stark truth: Unless you start *now*, *today* and get your act together, you will soon complete the eight billionth life of third-rate mediocrity, non-achievement, boredom and poverty since the stone age.

You know that giant counter outside MacDonalds' HQ which counts up the number of burgers served world-wide to date? I want one of those. It would be fifty feet by ten feet and mounted one hundred feet in the air. It would be linked into the world's funeral parlours and proclaim in giant illuminated digits the number of people who so far have died broke, unhappy, and unfulfilled. It would tick up relentlessly, the units digit would be a blur (about three thousand people die every second, world-wide). Every thousandth count, if you were quick, you would notice it appear to miss a beat. That's the one who got away. The happy, fulfilled goal-directed person who just passed away with a smile on his or her lips!

Will you be this person? Or will you join the teeming billions of the forgotten? Will you live a life of quiet desperation, frustration, poverty and hopelessness? Is this what you want? Are you prepared to settle for being mediocre? Is 'third-rate' good enough for you? Are you content with being just another nonentity in the faceless billions?

No? Then you're with me and I can help you.

The Four Stages to Success

There are four stages to living a life of power, wealth and passion.

I am not talking about a life of mediocrity and frustration. This is not what I teach. This is not what I am. A life of power means that you fulfil your life's dream with a style that makes an impact, and not in some insignificant way which leaves hardly a ripple on the pond. If you want to make ripples, chuck in a boulder, not the smallest pebble you can find. A life of passion means that you have guts, determination and you put some energy behind your chosen life-dream. You don't approach it as an apologetic, weak, humble, limp-wristed milksop. For the men, that means you've got to have *balls*. For the women, that means you've got to have some feminine *grit*. Two qualities which are sadly lacking in people today.

So, you want to become wealthy and make ten million or so? What action do you need to take? Here are the four stages which every self-made millionaire has passed through. Consider them to be initiation tests if you like. In this section I am going to be a little tough on you because, let's face it, you need a drill sergeant to get you moving otherwise you would have done it yourself long ago. So, for the moment, if you will indulge me, I am that drill sergeant.

Stage One

The first stage is becoming completely debt-free, including your mortgage if you have one. I have written about this at length in my Inner Circle materials, and so I will not duplicate that material here. I just want to say that this is the most essential task for every thinking humanoid (that means you) to complete as a matter of extreme urgency.

If you are unable to do this, then you are making the following statement: *"I came into this world with nothing. Despite countless years of work I have been unable to create a single penny of surplus. My entire life's efforts produced a negative balance, not a positive one, so I borrowed the efforts of others and spent them on my own comfort. I will probably die without even being able to repay these people."*

Isn't that statement the truth? Isn't that really the situation when stripped of its gloss and spin?

What a statement. What a way to live a life.

In case you had the slightest doubt, this is not a life of power and passion. This is the life of a poor, helpless, weak invalid who cannot even feed, house and clothe himself by his own efforts - they must borrow the efforts others in order to achieve this!

Put like that - which is the honest truth, not some condescending excuse - it sounds like a "damned poor show" as the old army colonels might have said. So stage one - the absolute minimum you must do as a self-respecting human - is to become completely debt-free.

How? I don't care how. *Just do it.* If you think I'm being hard on you, you're right! We're not discussing knitting patterns here. Of course it's hard! You have years of waste, self-indulgence, wrong thinking and downright laziness to put right. You can't do this in five minutes. Is this too tough for you? Then pay the penalty - become one more digit on the counter...

I am talking here about the ordinary debts we run up in life to buy a whole skip-full of junk which we think we need. The exception is debt incurred to make you wealthy - for example a mortgage on an industrial unit which you rent out, or a block of flats, or a business development loan. This is the sensible use of Other People's Money (OPM) to make you wealthy. When you are entirely debt-free, including mortgage, you are one rung up from the absolute lowest. You are still a flat-broke slave with zero personal power and little freedom. Why? Because you must work for your food, clothing, telephone, petrol, gas, electricity etc., etc. You have absolutely no choice in this. Your only choice is which master to slave for. After 40+ hours of slavery, you don't feel much like being creative or fulfilling your potential, right? It's the truth. So consider yourself one up from a beast of burden. Needless to say, someone with personal power gets to choose exactly how they spend their time each day.

Stage Two

The next step is to become financially independent.

What do I mean by this? First you decide on whatever level of pauper's existence you call a 'lifestyle' and work out how much money you need per year to maintain this level of squalor. Then you amass enough capital, invest it, and use the interest (etc.) to pay yourself this pittance each year. For example, if you need £20,000 minimum a year to survive, then you need roughly half a million in the bank, allowing for tax on interest paid, to realise this figure. If you need £40,000 a year then you need a million. These are just rough figures to give you the general principle.

If you think you've made it with a lousy million then you're wrong! You are still barely solvent. All you have done is to un-manacle your arms and legs from the cell wall, and walk away a free man or woman. You are merely *free*. Touch the capital and you immediately become a slave again. You are not rich, fulfilled, actualised or anything remotely like these things. You have merely been handed your certificate of freedom by the master, and are walking away from the plantation, down the dirt-track road into the unknown, swinging your bundle over your shoulder. Your lifestyle (£40,000 a year) is almost the bare minimum required for civilised existence. You have a modest house, a small car and a few sticks of furniture. You can eat out now and then - but not in good restaurants. You can buy new clothes occasionally - but not the best. You can go on holiday for two weeks - a package holiday, nothing special.

In short, you're bumping along just above the absolute bottom.

In case you hadn't guessed, I'm yanking your ceilings way, way higher than the cramped and lowly hovel you are prepared to crouch in! With a million pounds you are just starting on life's real journey. Whilst not small change, a million pounds is a very modest amount of money indeed - just enough to buy you your freedom and live a modest lifestyle without having to work.

Stage Three

This is where you accumulate about three million pounds - it varies from person to person.

Why three million?

Well, you need about one million to make you financially independent as discussed in stage two. Then you need another million to buy yourself lots of silly toys so that you can get all of this garbage out of your system. With a spare million, most rational people will rapidly run out of toys to buy. You want a decent house? Done. Interior designed? Okay. A Porsche? A Merc? A Range Rover? Have all three. Suits, dresses, shoes? Small change. We haven't spent a million yet! Umm... now you're struggling. A Rolex? A villa in a holiday resort? Done. There's still a hundred grand left in change!

The point is, the second million will sort you out for everything your heart could desire. Only a lottery-winning 'loadsamoney' moron would have six Rolexes up each arm and thirty cars!

On the subject of the lottery, do you know why many of the winners are miserable when interviewed a year later? It's because money, in itself, doesn't guarantee happiness. Money is an enabling force. In other words it empowers you to fulfil your potential. The happiness comes not from the material possessions - these give a quick fix or drug-like high which soon passes. No, the happiness comes from leading a worthwhile life and producing something of quality and value. Sitting around in a mansion and staring at your Porsche will not make you happy. Starting a bat preservation colony, buying a recording studio and writing songs, designing a museum of vintage cars, rebuilding steam locomotives... anything which you deem as your important life-work... this is what makes you happy. Money allows you to do it because it frees you from the need to work for a living and it allows you to do it in style and comfort. That is what getting wealthy is really all about.

Notice that even with this two million you have achieved nothing of value. All you have done is to become a free man or woman and buy yourself some toys. Big deal!

The third million elevates your subsistence-level income obtained from the first million, up to something sensible, but still not even close to being rich. Investing two million pounds will yield about £80,000 a year after tax - the sort of salary enjoyed by thousands of senior directors, doctors, lawyers and so on. Not one of these people would describe themselves as rich. With your house, furniture and cars all paid for, you can live very comfortably - but not extravagantly - on this level of money, but it is by no means what you would call wealthy.

Why would anyone want more than three million?

Why does Richard Branson get up in the morning? Why does Paul McCartney keep writing songs (I wish he'd stop)? Why doesn't Bill Gates pack it all in? After all, they've got loads of money, right? Are they just greedy, money-grubbing people who can't get enough?

No. They have all passed into stage four - the real point of life. The point which few people ever glimpse because most people spend their entire lifetime in a panic-stricken struggle to raise enough money to pay the gas bill.

Stage Four

So what is stage four?

If you have selected this powerful route it is nothing less than the noble purpose of your life. The real reason that you exist. The noblest struggle in which a man or woman of integrity can engage. It is nothing more or less than the struggle to be all you can be as a person. To live a life of power and passion in the pursuit of your dreams - whatever they are.

Every person is unique and has, if they did but realise it, a special set of talents and abilities not possessed by another living soul in that exact combination. The purpose of a powerful life is to become free - first debt-free, then financially independent - and then to follow your dream.

Becoming wealthy has little to do with buying a bunch of silly toys. You have to be a very sad individual if this is the limit of your imagination. How much champagne can you drink? How many Rolexes do you need? How big a wardrobe of clothes will satisfy you? This is all junk. They are toys - harmless baubles to amuse us for five minutes.

Attaining these toys is not the purpose of a noble life.

Once you are free from the crippling burden of debt and then amass enough funds to release yourself from the treadmill, then and only then is your spirit released and your true, inner self allowed fully to blossom. The money is for following your dream with power. The more money you have, the bigger the dream you can actualise. The smaller your pot of funds, the smaller and more insignificant must be the dream you can make manifest here on earth.

Richard Branson and Bill Gates do not get out of bed in order to make another £10 million. (Legal Notice: Neither I, nor my publishers are in any way implying that Bill and Richard were in bed *together...*). They both have a dream which they are following with passion. The money they make on each project allows them to dream bigger the next time. The limits to a man or woman's dreams are mainly self-imposed.

The goal is simply to be all you can possibly be. This is enough. This single goal encompasses all others. There is no 'retirement' - you can't retire from life until what? Until you die. The 'retire at 65' mentality is for the lost and poverty-stricken - the digits on the counter - not for you.

You will die in the pursuit of ever larger dreams and goals - this is how to live a noble life. What is the alternative to this superb and inspiring vision of power? To 'retire' at 65, flip magazines and do a bit of gardening? To take a day-trip to Shoreham on Sea? To watch a bit more TV? Is this the noble human purpose? Hardly.

I know it's hard to dream when you're tired. It is tough to have passion when you're struggling to pay the rent or mortgage. This is why you must take action and vow to break free of the treadmill. If you want the life I have been describing, then you must swear now, by all that is holy and sacred to you, that you will not rest until you have achieved it. I can't *give* you the balls and the grit - I can only try to inspire you. There is a limit to what I can do with printed words on a page. I can try to arouse you from your slumber and make you see that time is running out for you.

Ultimately though, if you think this is too hard and you haven't got any fight, there is only one course left for you to follow. Resign yourself to a life of third-rate mediocrity. Accept that you will never achieve anything significant. Admit that you will die broke and embarrassed. Abandon your dreams. Stop talking about becoming rich and achieving great things - these are just meaningless words which you do not believe in; you are deceiving yourself and making others laugh at you. Settle for less. Be like everybody else. Sink into the enfolding arms of the warm masses. There is some comfort there. Mediocrity is reassuring.

If this last paragraph fills you with dread (I could hardly bring myself to write it) then you know the alternative.

Fight.

Fight with every ounce of your strength and determination. Vow to yourself that one day you will be somebody, that you will achieve something of note; that you will become wealthy and use the money in the pursuit of your unique dream; that you will leave the planet a better, a richer, a more wonderful place than when you arrived all those years ago as a new-born infant. Think like Abraham Lincoln did: *"I do the best I know how, the very best I can; and I mean to keep on doing it to the end. If the end brings me out all right, what is said against me will not amount to anything. If the end brings me out all wrong, ten angels swearing I was right would make no difference."*

The Power Day

This 'secret' of taking action is so critical that I want to get you kick-started immediately with an amazing technique which I developed some years ago. I call it the Power Day and if you try this, it will absolutely convince you once and for all of the power of taking action instead of just talking about action.

A Power Day is one full day in which you vow to test your will against the inertia of the universe. This is not a recipe for daily living. You should have a Power Day about once every month.

It is quite incredible what you can achieve if you turn the full force of your will upon the problem and shatter inertia. I have proved this for myself on many occasions. Here's what you do:

Choose a full day in which you will not be disturbed. This is a sixteen hour period from 8 a.m. until midnight. This will be a tiring day for you, and that's an understatement. Before you start this day, you write on a piece of paper a list of things you want to achieve in this day. The list should include items which would usually take one or more *weeks* of normal 'procrasto-time.' I always ensure that my list includes:

1. One or two life-changing jobs which I have been putting off starting for the last few months (or years).
2. Some practical jobs of the 'clear out guttering' variety.
3. Some short ten minute jobs.
4. Some longer (one hour or so) jobs.
5. Some creative work.
6. Some intellectual work.
7. Some energetic practical work (cleaning, putting up shelves, etc.)

The point is that any one of these items would normally be your allotted task for a day or two. But a Power Day is not like that. During this day, it's you versus the inertia of the universe - and you are going to win.

In your Power Day, the sheer force of your willpower will boost you through these tasks. You do not rest. You work at full speed, but on a variety of jobs, grabbing a sandwich on the run. No procrastination. No endless cups of coffee, long baths or TV programmes. You work steadily through your list.

The trick to getting through is to vary the work. Break up the difficult life-changing tasks (these are nearly always the creative tasks) with some menial job like clearing leaves off the patio.

Rotate tasks. The point of this is not that you must finish everything (although you'll be startled at what you manage to complete!) but to keep working (taking action) until you fall exhausted into bed at midnight. You will be tired, but very happy. You will also have learned an important lesson about the raw power of taking action.

Keep pushing through. When you have completed one task, don't take time to congratulate yourself or relax - move right on to the next one, then the next.

If you are bogged down by spouse, family, dogs and cats, then take a day off work and book yourself into a cheap local hotel for 24 hours. If your family won't give you a day off, change your family!

During that one day, you will have accomplished more than you would normally do in one month. You will have proved to yourself the results of focusing your will and overcoming inertia. More importantly, you will have started those vital life-changing tasks which are the equivalent of course changes. Try this idea - it really works.

Like you, I am ruled by inertia. I succeed only because I have learned various tricks (like the Power Day) to overcome inertia.

I have found almost no limits to this technique. Let me give you an example. It has always been one of my many ambitions to write a hit song. I have dabbled with this for many years and I some time ago I wrote half the song and then spent six months tripping over it on a daily basis, thinking every day: "I must finish that song."

Does this sound familiar? Does it have a resonance with something in your life? So during my next Power Day, amongst the many things I wrote on the list was 'Finish the goddamned song.'

Now I think you will agree that writing a hit song or even half of one, would occupy most people for a week. But that was one of about sixteen items on my list of tasks to do in one day. I did all sixteen things with time to spare!

Concerning the song, here's how I did it. I used a little known and esoteric technique for producing work. Do you want to know what it was?

I started the job and didn't get up until it was finished.

Spooky stuff, right?

Songs (books, plays, etc.) don't get written by drinking tea, watching TV, 'waiting' for inspiration, messing around, chatting on the telephone or going for a walk.

When I had finished the song, I pushed on immediately. I did not sit back and congratulate myself (not on a Power Day). I immediately carried on to the next task - typesetting the music and lyric. A good friend of mine has the capability of doing this and so when did I call him? A few days later? Next week? No. I called him *immediately*. I took the draft around *immediately*. The great news was he was free and could do it *immediately*.

Surely writing the song and typesetting it in one day is enough, already? Time to watch some TV or flip through a magazine, right? You are joking, I hope? It was only eleven o'clock in the morning! Yes, that song which had waited six months, was completed in around two hours. So, I called some demo studios and told them about the song. I got them all set up to record it. Then I called some people in the music business and arranged to come and play them the demo. Next I recorded the song with me singing it (believe me, you don't want to hear this) onto cassette to send to the demo companies for them to make a decent demo tape. Then I addressed the jiffy bags. That's all I could do until the typeset music came back - which it did at eleven p.m. that night. Did I go to bed? Forget it. I went to the office, photocopied the music and posted it to the demo houses at midnight!

From 12 noon until eleven that night, I rattled off the other fourteen jobs, one of which was to complete the outline for a children's book I am trying to write. Get the idea? In one day I had taken two major steps towards 'money trees' in the future (children's books and music) and cleared up fourteen jobs which had been hanging around for weeks or months.

Remember, you don't have to be a 'one shot' genius marksman. I certainly am not a genius, I can promise you that. The person who hits the target is often the one who fires enough shots - some of them wild. In a fire-fight situation I was taught by my instructor to forget about fancy postures and accurate shooting, just get your head down and return fire as rapidly as possible. This is not a bad analogy for success. Get your head down and fire as rapidly as possible! Your 'bullets' of course, are your creative output.

Think what you could achieve during a Power Day!

I want you to schedule a Power Day right now in order for you to convince yourself about the raw power of taking action. You will be startled by the results, I can promise you.

Chapter Eight
You Must Know When to Stop

"The Wise Person Decides How Much is 'Enough' Before Setting Foot on the Path to Riches."

Now we arrive at the deepest secret of happiness associated with wealth. Also, this is the most difficult initiation test of all seven. Yes, knowing when to stop is actually more difficult than making it in the first place!

Remember one thing. The aim in life is to be happy. Money is one way (yes, a big way) in which you can achieve happiness, but don't lose sight of the fact that it is happiness you are after as a final goal, not money.

If you ever make any real money you will be so caught up in your astonishing success that you will find it very hard to quit. You will be tempted to work harder and faster to get more whilst the going is good. Then, if you hit a lean time, you will work harder and faster to try and get back what you have lost. In short, you will always be working harder and faster. Knowing when enough is enough is *the* most difficult challenge you will ever face.

Most people do not face this challenge because they rarely make enough to live on and almost never create a surplus. However, it is useful to ask yourself the question at any stage of your life, even if 'flat broke' as I hope to prove.

This is one of life's big questions, and I believe it would help you to try and answer it right now. In this single question I believe is embodied the spirit of the next thousand years - no small claim!

What is the question?

"Do You Have Enough?"

Strange question! Perhaps you're thinking "enough of what?" Or even, "what is he talking about?"

I have deliberately phrased the question in this simple form. You know what I'm talking about. You know what the question means. So I would like you to close your eyes for a moment, and let the question work its magic, before I elaborate and spoil its simple power.

Now I will answer your question, "enough of what?" I mean enough money, enough material possessions, enough 'things.' And before you answer a resounding "No - that's why I bought this book!" let me tell you some interesting facts about your current level of wealth. (I have accounted for inflation in these statistics.)

Wealth Fact #1

You are approximately one thousand times richer than the average ancient Egyptian, ignoring Pharaohs - you are only a mere fifty times richer than a Pharaoh. Of course you don't have the piles of gold they had, but that's not the point. The point is what they could and did buy with that gold, which was mainly slave-power. It has been estimated that modern inventions such as the motor car, washing machines, dishwashers, etc. are the equivalent of owning one thousand slaves, making you wealthier now (whatever your level of poverty) than the kings of the ancient world.

But...are you fifty times happier than a Pharaoh? Are you one thousand times happier than the average ancient Egyptian?

Are you even *as* happy as they were?

Wealth Fact #2

You are about three hundred times richer than the average ancient Briton living at the start of the first millennium; i.e. the year AD 1. You are an estimated thirty times richer than the wealthiest king or lord of that era. By richer, I mean your access to clean wholesome food, potable drinking water, transport, power, medicine, shelter, clothing and labour-saving devices, to mention only a few things. Stagnant piles of loot stacked up in a warehouse are not riches, any more than ten million in a Swiss bank account which is never touched is 'money.' Wealth is only meaningful if it is used.

Wealth Fact #3

You are an estimated one hundred times richer than the average Briton living at about the time of the Battle of Hastings, i.e. at around the start of the second millennium, the year AD 1066. You are ten times wealthier than the richest man on the planet one thousand years ago.

I am not including land ownership in these statistics. The mere ownership of land is not wealth: riches are measured in what the land produces. To prove this point, let me hereby grant you 100% ownership, absolute, of the planet Pluto - all ten trillion acres. You own the entire planet. Congratulations! Has it improved your level of wealth by even 1%? No, because it produces nothing.

Are you one hundred times happier than someone from 1066? Are you even *as* happy?

Wealth Fact #4

You are fifty times more wealthy than the average peasant living in the year 1500. Life was hard back then, but are you fifty times happier than they were? I doubt this very much. Are you even *as* happy? I wonder...

Wealth Fact #5

You are thirty times more wealthy than the average Englishman or woman living in 18th-century Britain.

Wealth Fact #6

You are twenty times more wealthy than the average Victorian. Looked at another way, you have the equivalent today of twenty Victorian servants working for you. A Victorian household with twenty staff would most definitely have been owned only by the superrich.

Wealth Fact #7

On average you are likely to be five time richer than your granddad. Are you five times happier than he was?

Wealth Fact #8

On average, you are likely to be twice as wealthy as your own parents, although this depends on your age. If you are 18, it will not apply. If you are 50, it almost certainly will. For example, think back to the thirties, forties, fifties, or sixties, whichever decade is closest to when you were growing up. Did each family have two cars? Mobile telephones? Dishwashers? Microwaves? Did your mom and dad take expensive foreign holidays, sometimes even more than one in a year? Did they wear expensive designer clothes? You get the idea. In the 1930s, which surely is only 'yesterday,' over 25 million Americans had no income whatsoever; only 1% of UK homes had a telephone; only 50% had electricity and nutrition was so poor that six out of ten men who applied for the army failed their basic "if you can stagger, you're in" medical test and could not join up.

Wealth Fact #9

You are already in the very top 1% of the world in terms of wealth. Most people on the planet still live on subsistence farms, carrying water from long distances, without sanitation or electricity. Are you happier than they are, on average?

At this point in the proceedings, I want to ask my question again:

"Do you have enough?"

Think about it. You are already *one thousand* times wealthier than an ancient Egyptian, *three hundred* times richer than someone living in AD1; *twenty times* wealthier than the average Victorian; *five times* wealthier than your grandfather and in the top 1% of wealthy people on the planet.

Do you have enough?

This is not a one-shot question, it is a question for life. You need to continuously ask yourself this from now until you die. If the answer is still "no," then I want to ask you a supplementary question which you need to answer, right now: "When do you think you *will* have enough?" I am not asking these questions for amusement only. I believe the answers hold one of the keys to your happiness for the rest of your life. Again, no small claim. Let me explain.

Welcome, Fellow Rat

Recently I've started to notice something. I have become aware of the incredible stress under which most people live their lives - myself included. People are working harder, faster and certainly under more stress that at any time in history. I agree that the labour is not usually hard physical toil, but still the average person is slaving away forty or fifty hours a week to make enough money to make ends meet - i.e. to sustain their 'poor' lifestyle which is twenty times wealthier than the average Victorian. Furthermore, they are not happy.

In general, we are all overworked, highly stressed and on a treadmill getting nowhere fast. It's the rat-race which was identified so long ago. Incredibly, although we are all approximately one thousand times wealthier than an ancient Egyptian, we feel broke. Most people are fighting a losing battle against a tide of debt and expenses which threaten to sweep them away if they do not keep their noses pressed firmly to the grindstone. Despite their huge wealth, in historical terms, many people are anxious and depressed by their 'poverty.'

This seems incredible, doesn't it? What on earth would an ancient Briton make of us if you brought him here in a time capsule?

He would see the clean, safe water on tap - it took him one full day each week of backbreaking labour just to get enough water, and that was brackish and flavoured with dead sheep; he would see the stunning abundance of food at almost give-away prices - you have to work just 24 hours a month to buy all the rich abundance of family food, he would have to work an average of 160 hours for some basic meat and bread. He would note your clean clothes and the dozens of different sets of clothing you owned - he owned one set and it was constantly filthy as there was no soap and no hot water. He would marvel at your health, your teeth, your longevity - his life expectancy was 30 years, his teeth were rotten stumps and people died all around him from disease and hunger.

I could go on about transport (he had none), opportunities (zero), education (crude), entertainment (sitting around a camp fire and telling Wild Boar jokes), but I also think he would be shocked at the level of unhappiness and stress we were all living under. He would legitimately ask why on earth we were all striving so hard when we had everything and more that we could possibly need.

Why, he would ask, did we not all feel incredibly wealthy and happy?

Well, let me ask you a few questions.

Do *you* feel extraordinarily wealthy?

Are *you* happy?

Do *you* have an almost stress-free life?

Do *you* have plenty of time to do the things you want to do, or are you always working to hold back the tidal wave?

Are *you* engaged in a constant struggle for more, more, more?

If so ... when do you think *you* will have enough?

Now please do not think for a moment that I am on some kind of anti-wealth, back-to-nature, tree-hugging crusade. Nothing could be further from the truth. I have not make any comment about how much 'enough' might be. This is for you to decide. It could be £50,000 or £100 million.

My task is to get you to think about the question, because the answer has profound implications for your happiness.

How Much is Enough?

To explain this, let me make a blunt statement:

Your greed is insatiable (mine too, of course). There is almost no limit to what you would want to possess. The only limit is the price you would be willing to pay to obtain it, and your imagination. To prove this, let us play a little game in which the price of anything you want is *zero*. I mean it will cost you nothing in cash terms or emotional terms and requires zero time or input from you to maintain. This, if you like, is the ultimate free lunch.

I'm getting my cheque book out. I have unlimited resources at my disposal. How large a cheque would you like, made out to you personally? Remember, it's free in every sense. No penalty, no tax, no hassle. It's yours to have and to spend on whatever you want. Shall we start the bidding at, say, £50,000? Remember, I really do have an unlimited account. How about a quarter of a million? You could buy a nice house with that, mortgage-free. Hopefully your imagination is not quite so shackled and you are already starting to think about a nice fat juicy cheque for a million pounds. No problem. It's not my money, and it's unlimited. Have what you want - there are no strings attached.

One million pounds will allow you to buy the house of your dreams, and the car(s) of your dreams. What's that? You'd rather have *ten* million pounds? Now you're talking. I was getting worried about you for a moment there. That's more like it. This will give you all the money you could ever need for the rest of your life. It would take care of your children and your grandchildren.

Enough?

Remember, it's free. All that is limiting you is your imagination...

Let's face facts, ten million pounds would not even buy you admission to the outer circle of the superrich. To tempt you further, and in case you think I was just kidding with that 'unlimited' promise, let me disclose that I have one hundred thousand million, billion pounds in this account, earmarked to give away - and you're first in the queue. You can have the lot, if you want, and I won't turn a hair, in fact you'd be doing me a favour as I could then close the account and stop worrying about it.

What would you do with it? Come on now! Think! You could buy your own country and run it the way you wanted to. You could own and run the entire United Kingdom or America or even (bwahahaha...) *the world!*

Why not? Your vision for the world can't be any worse than the current awful state it is in! Couldn't you do a better job if you had absolute power? How about being absolute ruler of the planet? How does that sound? But wait... the earth is just *one* planet in the solar system. How about owning a few other planets too? How about owning the entire Martian planet, and having the money to teraform it exactly as you want?

Your own world, and you as....*God*.

Now perhaps you dropped out somewhere on that continuum, possibly at the one million or ten million level?

Or perhaps you were with me to the end? I can tell you with absolute certainty that I definitely would be up for the job of Total Ruler of the Planet. No question. And it would be a better place than it is now! If you did drop out, it was because your imagination failed you. You simply could not imagine having more money or power than this.

Now back to reality...

Our Insatiable Greed

I hope I have proved that your greed (my greed, everybody's greed) is almost limitless if I make it a free lunch for you. Apart from your lack of imagination, the only thing which holds you back from owning the whole planet is something known as 'paying the price' which we discussed in Secret 5, chapter 6.

To remind you, everything has a price in time, effort, risk, stress and strain. There truly is no such thing as a free lunch. If you want £50 you have to pay the price (e.g. five hours work). If you want £20,000 each year, then the price is typically forty hours of your irreplaceable life each week working in a job you barely tolerate.

If you want one million pounds, the price is typically, ten solid years of 60-80 hour weeks; high stress, almost zero social life, poor family life and high personal and financial risk. That's about the going rate. You may get it cheaper, or it may cost you more.

If you want ten million pounds, the price is typically a lifetime spent in the fast lane as a top industrialist or entrepreneur. The price is active media coverage of your personal and corporate life; twenty or thirty years of 80 hour weeks; permanent stress; living in the 'white water' of a constantly changing market place and absolute devotion to your vision to the exclusion of almost everything else. You will have no real friends - you can never tell who your real friends are when you have this level of wealth; you will attract government surveillance - money equals power, governments cannot allow the drones to have too much personal power and so they become *very* interested in you when you make more than ten million.

If you want one hundred million or more, the price is everything associated with getting ten million, plus a slavering pack of press wolves, desperate to strip you down to the lowest common denominator. You will have many enemies both personal and political, some of which will actively want you terminated. For example, an estimated thirty million people world-wide detest Bill Gates and would spit straight into his face if they could only get in range. About 1,000 of these are crazy enough to murder him, given a chance and a clear shot. I am not joking here.

You will be unable to live anything approaching a normal life. You will not be allowed out on your own without bodyguards, and you will live in a heavily guarded fortress. Most people will loathe and despise you, no matter how much of your wealth you give away to charity as a token gesture. Even if you give away one billion pounds you will be despised and vilified for being mean - most people will just shrug and say "he can afford it."

That's the price, give or take.

Okay, so we're ready to pull a few threads together here.

Here are the facts as I see them:

1. You are already staggeringly wealthy compared with at any previous time in history, yet you are running harder, faster and under immense personal stress in order to get more. You don't know how much more, because you have never thought about it. I also humbly suggest you are not very happy.

2. Your greed is, to all intents and purposes, insatiable. This is not a moral judgement. It is simply a statement of fact about human beings. What you would like to have is limited only by your imagination, and your willingness to pay the price required to get it.

3. Given that there *is* a price to pay in time, effort, stress, emotion, and risk in order to obtain a given amount of wealth, any sensible person would ask themselves the very basic question: "How much is enough?" Or, put another way: "Do I have enough? If not, when will I have enough?"

The purpose of life is not to stack up money in the bank. Despite my pro-wealth stance and motivational materials I have never claimed this. The purpose of your short stay on the planet is, I believe, to be all you can be and to live a happy, fulfilled and balanced life. You need money to live a decent lifestyle, and depending on your vision, you need money to make your dreams a reality. More than this you do not need. If it was free, you would take it of course, so would I and rightly so. *But it isn't free.* Everyone must pay a price to obtain it.

When you ask yourself the simple question: "Do I have enough?" something almost magical happens. Many people describe a feeling of release - a sort of letting go. You might feel that you are finally able to drop a burden which you have been carrying all your life.

Whatever you feel, there are surely only three possible answers to this question:

1. I have more than enough.
2. I have exactly enough.
3. I do not have enough and am willing to pay the price to get more. I now need to ask myself: "So when *will* I have enough?"

To expand on these three answers:

1. "Now you bring it to my attention, I realise that I have more than enough. I am debt free, and have considerable savings, yet still I am working 60 hours a week in a high stress job. A lot of my money actually goes to pay for my high profile lifestyle which is required by the job. For example, I need to live close to my job and housing is very expensive in our area. If I moved, I could get a larger house for half the money. It costs a fortune to commute to work. My children are in private school. We pay a nanny to look after the children because my wife works as well. It's crazy. Why do I do it? I don't know. Probably because I've always done it. I guess it is just a habit. If I made certain life changes, I could work two or three days a week. We would have to move, and have a simpler lifestyle, but we are both so stressed at the moment, surely it could not be worse? I've realised one thing, I could easily make more money. I just need to work harder, faster or smarter. But I choose not to. That is a breakthrough for me. *I choose not to.* That is real power."

Could *you* live a simpler, lower stress life? Could you work less hard and live more simply, doing more of the things you want to do - whatever they are? Sure, you could easily make a lot more money, but how about considering the choice of not doing this? This book is all about you taking one of two choices; to become wealthy and pay the price, or to live a planned, simpler more balanced life. There is no right or wrong path, although I have my own preferences, naturally.

You know you can make more money by working harder, faster, longer, smarter. Nobody is denying your abilities. It's easy. But... why not consider the option of choosing not to do this? This means setting a limit on what you have - saying, in effect, "I have enough" and using the time you would have spent in striving for more, to do the other things you've always promised yourself you will do. This phenomenon is known as 'downshifting' and is sweeping across America. If this isn't an option for you right now, still you need to constantly be thinking about this option throughout your life.

Answer two:

2. "Yes, now you mention it, I have exactly enough at the moment. Of course, I would like more, and if it was free I would take it from you with thanks. But I know that in order to get more I need to sacrifice more of my life and I am not willing to do this. There are many other things I want to do with whatever time is left to me. I would rather do those than work harder, faster and take on yet more stress in order to accumulate more money. I am not willing to pay the price for higher financial rewards. Making more money is not difficult. There is plenty of overtime at work, and I could take a second job in the evenings. But I have taken a powerful decision in my life. I have decided that I have enough. I have chosen not to pursue yet more money."

Could *you* be at peace with your current level of wealth? Taking such a decision frees you from the constant struggle to make more. It frees you from the nagging guilt about not starting your own business, or expanding your current one. It saves you having to buy more books like this, and tapes and seminars...

Answer three:

3. "No, I do not have enough. I want more - a lot more. I am willing to pay the price. If that means ten or twenty years of constant struggle to make a couple of million, then that's what I'll do. I have asked myself the question: "when will I have enough?" and I have an answer. I do not want to struggle in a high-stress environment forever, accumulating cash until I die. I want a four-bedroom detached house (fully paid), a brand-new

Mercedes, and the equivalent of half a million pounds in today's money in the bank. That would mean I never have to work again. That's enough for me. If I can make half a million pounds, I know I could make one million or ten million for that matter. I have no doubt about this. But I have made a choice. I know what I want and I'm going to get it. I am willing to pay the price. I know what that price is, approximately. I also know how much is enough and this lets me know when to stop chasing wealth, and concentrate on many of the great things which life has to offer."

How about you?

If you desperately want more and are willing to pay the price, then great! I certainly did, and I paid the price too. But... what I didn't do was to ask myself the question: "When will I have enough?" I didn't even think about that. I just ploughed straight in, never raising my head to look at how far I had come. I had no real plan and no exit strategy. Let me be clear, we are talking exit strategies here. Exit from the rat-race, as it used to be called.

Work At Making Money Until You Drop?

Are you going to work at making money until you drop? If so, why? What is it all for? Only a fool would do this. So, if you are not going to work until you drop, *when* are you going to stop, or cut back? I don't mean stop living and atrophy, I mean stop accumulating cash. Answer: When you have 'enough' - so you need to know what 'enough' is for you, bearing in mind the price.

Also, you need to think about what else you want to do with your life, if anything. And this is a problem for many people. We are all so conditioned to work until we drop that we have given little thought to what else we want to do with our lives. Perhaps now is the time for you to think a little about this?

The best way to get wealthy is to start a business, but you should not start or run a business unless you have a clear answer to the questions: "*When* do I get out? *When* will I have enough?" Running a business is all about making maximum money in minimum time, then selling out or closing down and getting yourself a real life! If your business is also your passion, as I have recommended, then you might never actually close it down, but it becomes more of a hobby than a driving force which dictates your life.

The Stasis Concept

If you run your own business, no matter how large or small, I want you to at least consider the following proposal, which, as far as I am aware, is uniquely my own idea:

All businesses need to expand, otherwise they are dead, right?

Wrong! I don't believe this. When you expand your business, two things happen:

1. You run harder and faster and pile on the stress both for you and your employees.

2. You don't make any money because you plough every penny back in to fuel the expansion. Worse, you frequently go into heavy debt to fund the expansion. It's all 'jam tomorrow.'

If you continue this process, you are pinning all your hopes on selling the business some way down the line, and cashing in your chips. This may, or may not happen. Most times it doesn't happen due to a variety of factors. Markets change, people change. You find you have this huge gaping mouth to feed every month. You wake up one morning and realise you need to make £100,000 each month just to meet payroll and other bills. You run faster and faster, growing all the time. New staff, new premises, new products, new territories, take-overs, mergers. And all with little profit because of the expansion drive.

Now if this is what turns you on, then go for it. I know a few people who have made many millions doing just this. For each of those, I know twenty who *thought* they would make millions, but lost everything.

So how about this: Why not run a business which *doesn't* expand? A business in which you choose not to make ever *increasing* amounts of money, even though you could - easily. This is a business which makes a great deal of money each year, but does not expand. It changes, but does not get larger. I have named this concept 'stasis.'

For example, let's say you currently turn over £1 million and make £150,000 profit - the exact figures are not relevant. Your business might be ten times larger than this, or one tenth as large. Let's say you decide *always* to do this, give or take 10%, and ignoring inflation, for the next few years at least.

Supposing you make a deliberate decision not to grow. Why? Because you have enough, and the price of growing is just too high a price to pay.

Suppose you could run this company working three days a week instead of six? Wow! Think what you could do with the spare time! Supposing this made you happier, less stressed and a far better manager/entrepreneur during the three days you worked?

Could you turnover £2 million and make £300,000? Sure. There is no question, but... suppose you decide not to? You take a conscious decision that £150,000 a year income is enough for you. Yes you'd take £300,000 if it was free, but you know it isn't free. There's a price to pay in extra hours, extra stress, extra work and sacrifice of your irreplaceable life. What an amazing decision to make! During the course of a typical business year, all sorts of projects arise with the potential to make money - but you turn them all down! Why? Because they would push your turnover above the preset £1 million mark, and you've decided not to do this. You are not going to run after every project just because it could make more money for you.

The analogy is deciding not to take an evening job down the pub in addition to your day job, because you have decided that you already have enough. Could you make extra cash working down the pub? Sure. But the price is long hours and evenings away from the family, and you have chosen not to go for this.

The Money Lever

This thought process alters the way you view your business or your job. You now correctly view it simply as a moneymaking machine. You pull a heavy lever, and out comes a crisp £10 note. You pull the lever again and out pops another. Great! So what are you going to do?:

1) Pull the lever repeatedly, morning, noon and night for 30 years, never even counting the huge pile of notes, until you drop dead of a heart attack one day, beside a large pile of three million pounds in crisp tenners.

2) Sit back and think for a moment. Think to yourself something like this: "I have a neat little money making machine here. It could provide me with 'enough' if I operate the lever 8 hours a day, for 3 days a week. Sure, I *could* operate the lever six days a week for ten hours a day, and I would definitely get more money, but I am going to choose not to do this. I want to do a lot of other things in my life instead of pulling that lever. If I play this right, I can keep this money-machine ticking for a decade or more with minimal effort on my part."

So I want you to think carefully about your working life and your plans. It's a new millennium and a new deal. You're going to live a lot longer than anyone at any previous time in history. It's going to be even easier for you to make 'enough.' Why not have a careful think about what 'enough' might be for you, and then formulate a definite plan to get this, and no more? Meanwhile, you need to do a lot of work on what it is you are *really* on the planet for, and go and do it!

Chapter Nine
The Secret of Happiness

"To Allow Yourself to be Happy is the Greatest Wisdom There is."

Since we have been discussing happiness in the last chapter, I thought I would just toss in the ultimate secret of happiness for you as a sort of free bonus!

Yes, that Holy Grail which has eluded wise men throughout the ages, is yours, free in the closing pages of this book!

You might like to know that the secret of happiness can be explained in just eight words and is, in fact, quite mundane. It does not involve meditation, drugs or self-flagellation. Each of the eight words is worth one million pounds, but here they are, free:

Tomorrow, Today, Live For Better
Working a Whilst

What? You can't make sense of that? I gave you the words for free, but the correct *order* is going to cost you plenty...

Pause, whilst the anagram-freaks try to work it out for themselves....

Got it? No? Okay you'll have to read on...

Now the price for my arranging the words for you is about ten minutes of your time to read this section carefully, because it has important implications for your happiness.

The first thing I want to say is that the human psyche - your psyche - is a very delicate thing indeed - and can be badly damaged, particularly during your early years, by what would outwardly seem to be 'not very much.'

Put another way, your mind is an incredibly delicate and subtle mechanism - a finely tuned and highly sensitive instrument. So delicate is this wonderful apparatus, that it is flat-out impossible to grow up without some damage to its mechanism.

Moderate damage is normal and severe damage is common.

Please read that last sentence again.

I would say that 100% of people - that's *everyone* - has moderate damage to their psyche, and about one in three have severe damage. I am talking about damage caused by a normal upbringing, not an abused upbringing. Thankfully abuse is not the norm, but more importantly, the psyche is damaged by numerous small incidents throughout your childhood where you didn't get exactly *what* you needed, exactly *when* you needed it.

Parents are, after all, people. They are neither omniscient nor telepathic. They do their absolute best, working from the basis of their own damaged psyches.

And so the cycle continues...

Now the point here is that because everyone is damaged, this means that everyone exhibits symptoms of 'mental disturbance' during, and often throughout, their lives. I'm talking 100% of people here. Such symptoms include:

1. Anxiety.
2. Depression.
3. Sleeplessness.
4. Irrational fear/panic attacks.
5. Feelings of worthlessness, insecurity, pointlessness.
6. Suicidal thoughts.
7. Substance abuse (particularly alcohol which is a wonderful anaesthetic for the harshness of life).
8. Irrational anger/impatience/irritation.
9. Worry.

Because everyone experiences some or all of these on a scale of mild to severe, everyone pretends that they don't experience these things and we all play this ridiculous game in which we pretend it's just other people who have problems, not us.

I have talked to hundreds of people from paupers to billionaires. Scratch the surface and what do you get? The same old human-being we all are. The damaged psyche resulting in some or all of the negative symptoms I have listed.

I find this immensely comforting. The real problem about feeling down on life is when you think it's only *you* who feels like this, and that everyone else is having a great time counting their loot. If you can really take on board what I am telling you here, that everyone is a seething mass of insecurity, angst, unfinished business and emotional turmoil, then I think that helps a great deal.

It's called 'the human condition' and comes about as a result of us all having such an immensely delicate psychology. We are about as equipped psychologically to handle the 'slings and arrows' of life as a butterfly is to handle a force ten storm.

Every human on the planet is brave beyond measure. Forget 'bravery in the face of enemy fire.' That's just one sort of bravery and anyway, most soldiers didn't have a choice about going over the top. I'm talking real bravery of the sort you show every morning. You get up and face the world again. You against the world. And it's as much a battle today as it ever was. Labour-saving devices make very little difference. Do you have lots and lots of leisure time because you own a 'fridge, a washing machine and a dishwasher? No? I thought not. It's the same old struggle by the same old human beings.

There is a danger in writing (and reading) a motivational, go-get-'em, kick-ass 'secrets of the millionaires' book because it encourages the sort of polarisation I was talking about earlier. You can easily think something like: "Yeah, it's as I suspected, everyone *else* is happy and making great money, it's only me who cannot achieve anything of note. I'm all alone. Everyone else is so happy and well adjusted..."

I'm telling you now, in as plain a way as I can say, that everyone on the planet is more or less screwed-up because of the way we are, and the way the world is. You just cannot avoid the damage.

You have to accept it, patch up what you can and live with the rest. So what can you do to increase your chance of happiness?

Live Today

The first part of the key to happiness is to live today.

That means you must try to live in the present moment, experiencing what is happening right now to you, good or bad.

This is it. This *is* your life. This is not a dress-rehearsal. But the twist here is to set this in the context of everything I have just said. Recognise that angst and upset are part of the human condition, experienced by everyone. This is just what it is to be a human being. We are all like this.

Why? Because from baby to teenager we had thousands of needs, most of which were met, many of which were not. Each time a need was not met (particularly from early childhood) it caused psychological damage, sometimes mild, sometimes serious.

The brain is highly adaptive and most damage can be routed around in order to allow the organism to continue functioning, albeit at a slightly reduced capacity. We develop coping strategies the most effective of which is just good old-fashioned, plain avoidance - we simply avoid the people and situations which cause the emotional pain and this stops us living life in all of its full colour.

When I say "live today" I'm not talking about some blissed-out, tree-hugging hippie who tries permanently to empty his mind in order to contact the 'now.' I'm talking about experiencing *today* with all of its upsets, angers, joys and sorrows. Just riding the wild bronco of life and not letting that sucker kick you off.

And when, as I often do, you experience a moment of intense pleasure, I want you to think to yourself: "This is as good as it gets." And it's true. These moments are as good as it gets.

Life is hard. Just as hard today, in its own way, as it ever was. Perhaps not as hard on us physically, but a lot harder on us mentally. That's why we're not a lot happier now than in 1400 - to pick a year at random.

So I want you to snatch happiness when it comes to you, like a drowning man or woman seizing the proverbial straw. This is what it means to 'live today. '

The alternative is to ignore the minor day-to-day happiness and always be thinking some version of*: "I'll be happy tomorrow, when..."* (I have money, I get a girlfriend, I move from this bad area, I get myself a new car...)

You won't.

Or to think: *"How can I possibly be happy now when..."* - and then insert your own unique bit of current misery, angst, depression, anxiety, panic or fear. The error here is to think that one day you'll be totally free of these things, and *then* you can be happy.

You won't. It's how we all are - riddled with this stuff. It's what makes us all human. It's what it *means* to be human. I'd go so far as to say that a person without a smattering of these things would be a flat, lifeless and intensely boring automaton. It is the degree of your angst which is important.

Zero makes you dull as ditch water.

A sprinkling makes you human and still allows for a lot of happiness. A moderate level makes you interesting, quirky and able to cope mostly with life, but like a semi-active volcano, side-shoots of lava keep erupting and causing turmoil in your life - you need to spend some time fixing the damage, otherwise you may erupt one day.

A lot, and you are mostly immobilised in life and unable to function. Happiness is denied to you and all of your efforts should be expended in therapy to repair the worst of the damage, before you can go on. You are constantly depressed, frightened and anxious.

As an analogy, imagine a football team in immaculate, Persil-white strip, nancying around the field avoiding getting grass-stains on their clean white socks. They would be a bit of a disappointment, really. They don't want to get too involved in the game in case they get mud on their shorts or a bruise from that big, nasty old ball. Who wants to watch them? Who cares? They are not fully engaged with the game.

A football team whose players are muddied, bruised and riled are an altogether more interesting spectacle. They'll be fighting with passion and determination, taking daring risks, sometimes winning some ground, sometimes losing some ground, but always entirely absorbed in the game and playing right now in the present moment.

But a team who are injured, demoralised, cold and wet need to do one thing - retire from the field, get some serious rest, bandage their cuts and recuperate. There is no point in their playing any longer. In fact, they *can't* play. Their minds are not on the game, but fully absorbed with their pain and humiliation.

So, you see, the trick is to grab the happiness, now, in spite of any current misery from your worry list.

A Brighter Future

The final part of the key to happiness is: "Whilst working for a better tomorrow." So the whole secret is:
"Live Today Whilst Working For A Better Tomorrow."

Why not write this out on a 3" x 5" card and put it somewhere you will see it each day? It's not a bad idea.

First, you grab every single morsel of happiness which comes your way, despite your perfectly normal negative feelings which you now know are part of the human condition and which *everyone* experiences.

Next, you must realise that everything you are today and everything you own today is a direct result of your past decisions. Decisions which you took, either consciously, or by default. Nobody else is to blame here. But once again I find this immensely comforting, because the power is in your hands to change the future, you don't have to wait for someone else to change it for you.

If your present life is a result of your past decisions, then the future is created by your present decisions, and boy is that true!

So you should be constantly working and scheming so that your future (which will come around soon enough) will be even better than your present. And you do this in spite of any angst and turmoil you might be feeling, just as you do it in spite of the fact that you have to breathe air and sleep seven hours each night.

Now if you recognise yourself in the 'moderate' or 'severe' category of emotional turmoil, then part of the process of planning for a better tomorrow involves working on yourself, perhaps through therapy, counselling or talking to trusted friends. By the way, you cannot do this alone or through introspection.

Think of this as urgent repairs to the ship's hull, without which the boat is in danger of going down. Only a fool would try to sail in such a boat without spending some time in dock to patch things up. Perhaps you've been in denial about the condition of this leaky old tub? Have you been bailing like a demon for the last few years whilst battling on through stormy seas, just about keeping afloat? This is a judgement only you can make.

But apart from the psychological work, there remains the real down and dirty work required right now, today, to make your future better for you and your family. I guess this is what separates the winners from the losers. Winners know they have to work *now* in order to get 'lucky' several years down the line and reap the rewards. Losers want the rewards right now and cannot make the link between now and the future. They have what I have often described as a 'Bunteresque' view of life (from Billy Bunter), hoping that something will turn up.

You can't live like that and be successful. You have to live your life on purpose, not by random chance. I cannot stress enough the importance of working for a better tomorrow despite any strong reasons why you feel you can't, such as:

1. The terrible state of the world.
2. Your deep emotional scars.
3. Your age (you feel it's too late).

Work gives direction, meaning and engages the brain. Idleness rots you from deep within.

I feel this is one of the most important issues and one of the hardest for me to write about. I guess the reason you bought this book is because I'm just a few steps ahead of you on the path to wealth, happiness and freedom, and through my writings, I pass along my views of the scenery, what you can expect and how to negotiate the obstacles you are about to meet.

The final thing in Pandora's box was... hope. And when you are working for a better tomorrow, you are reaching into that box for that last, most precious gift.

Conclusion

Immense wealth is within your grasp - but it won't be a simple ride.

Millions of people are wealthy and although it isn't an easy thing to get rich it is far from impossible.

Many chatter that they want to be rich, but few people have researched the factors required to achieve this. There are, indeed, several 'secrets' known to those who have fought their own way to the top of the mountain. If you have some aptitude and are willing to listen, you can learn these secrets for yourself and follow those 'lucky' ones to the dizzy heights.

The first thing you must have is a **firm belief that being rich is okay.** If you harbour any socialist leanings, then these will eventually sabotage your wealth-creating efforts, ensuring that you remain poor.

You must have a dream to act as a guiding beacon to lure you on when the going gets tough and the way ahead is dark. You cannot get rich by randomly selecting a field of endeavour for which you have no aptitude and even less interest. This is a ten or twenty year project; **it cannot and must not be a ten or twenty year prison sentence.** So you must do whatever it takes to unlock your secret dreams and passions. Hopefully others will share your passion and you can engage in commerce with them and make your fortune whilst having the time of your life.

One little trick used by all highly successful people is to have a battle-plan, sometimes called an action list or goal list. Life dreams are usually large and unwieldy and so the wise person knows how to break up these dreams into bite-sized chunks of a suitable size for our limited minds. **Winners set goals, losers never set goals.** It's that simple. Despite reading this advice fifty or a hundred times, **still some people will not write down their goals.**

Having written your goals and broken the large tasks down into simpler steps, now you **require discipline to keep you on track**, working through the list. Winners have this discipline. Losers wander aimlessly, become bored or distracted, have low frustration tolerance, give up easily and drift away. If I had to pick one single secret as the most important, it would be to cultivate a sense of discipline because from this, many other things follow.

When setting your goals, make sure you keep firmly in mind that **everything you obtain in this world has a price tag attached.** You must be willing to pay the price, otherwise you are only window-shopping and this means you are not serious about life, just browsing.

Until this point, mostly this is theory. Now it is time for action. **Above all, successful people are men and women of action.** They get their sleeves rolled up and get on with the task at hand. Unsuccessful people procrastinate and always want to do it 'tomorrow.' Of course, tomorrow never comes. The two main reasons for non-action are laziness and fear. The fear is usually fear of success or fear of change. We are all lazy, we all fear change. Winners are able to push through these negatives. Losers succumb to them.

Before you start out on this journey, **you need to have a clear idea about how much is enough**, otherwise you have no destination and your search becomes an endless quest. If you are not clear about your destination, how can you ever know when you have arrived? Also, making money, no matter how enjoyable, has a price tag associated with it. Ideally you want to minimise the time you spend doing this and so you must have a clear idea of how much you want. There is no point whatsoever in amassing riches, never enjoying the fruits of your labours, and dying a wealthy man or woman. **Money is an enabling force, not an end in itself.**

Finally, the journey is everything as there is only one, macabre destination which we all share. The last stop on the line is Grim Reaper Halt. Life is a process, not a product. So no matter what your current level of wealth, it is time for you to start mastering one of life's most difficult lessons and that is to be happy right here, right now whilst working towards a better tomorrow.

This book has been an attempt to get you to decide which of two paths in life you want to follow, and then for you actively to choose that path and live with your decision. One path is hard and stony. It rises steeply above you towards a distant mountain top. There is no guarantee of happiness on that mountain, but something calls you to it.

The second path is not so steep. It meanders through the valley, taking in some interesting scenery on the way. It leads nowhere in particular, but the journey is an interesting and pleasant one.

There is no right or wrong path. Legend has it that both paths eventually converge in a mysterious dark valley from which no traveller has ever returned...but that's just a legend.

Choose your path wisely. But do choose, do not drift.

I wish you the very best in your journey.

Printed in Great Britain
by Amazon